Introduc

Coed y Brenin, the King's Forest, cover
in Gwynedd and is managed by Forestr
Welsh Assembly Government. The forest
and Wen rivers and is bisected by the main
Trawsfynydd. Although still a working forest, Coed y Brenin was designated a forest
park during the 1990s and is now famed for its cycling trails and other recreational
facilities. A well designed Visitor Centre and café was opened north of Ganllwyd, just
off the A470, in 2006.

This book is intended to complement the network of walking trails in Coed y
Brenin already waymarked by Forestry Commission Wales. The area is renowned for
its spectacular mountain scenery (the wild Rhinog mountains lie to the west of the
forest and the remote peaks of Dduallt and Rhobell Fawr to the east), its river valleys
with their rapids and waterfalls, its gold mines and its remote farms. The Roman road,
Sarn Helen, passes through the forest on its way between the forts at Tomen y Mur,
near Trawsfynydd, and Brithdir, near Dolgellau. In addition, the attractive village of
Ganllwyd lies at the centre of the park.

The walks in this book vary in length and level of difficulty but can all be
undertaken by a reasonably fit person. Walking boots or strong shoes, and waterproof
clothing, are recommended for all of them. The six starting points for the walks were
chosen with the idea of giving the visitor as varied an experience of Coed y Brenin
and its topography as possible. Ganllwyd is the first of the starting points, with a
number of walks, some on National Trust land, exploring the waterfalls and hills
which surround the village. The Visitor Centre at Dolgefeiliau provides an excellent
introduction to the park, so a number of walks are based there. Both Ganllwyd and
Dolgefeiliau are readily accessible by public transport as they are served by Arriva bus
services (for details see **Walks 1** to **11**). The remaining four starting points require a car
using minor roads to the north and east of the forest.

The location of each route is shown on the back cover and a summary of the main
characteristics and approximate length of each is shown on a chart on the inside back
cover. An estimated duration is also given but allow longer in order to linger over the
many fine views and interesting places visited whilst on the walks. A weather forecast
for this area is available on 09068 232785 (charge) or at www.met-office.gov.uk.

Please note that Coed y Brenin is a busy mountain bike destination and that you
should take account of cyclists when walking in the forest. New trails may be created
after the publication of this book, while forestry operations and other Coed y Brenin
events may necessitate the temporary closure of sections of some routes. Up-to-date
information may be obtained from the Visitor Centre on 01341 440747.

Michael Burnett would like to thank the following for their advice and support in
the preparation of this book: Aled Thomas, Local Area Manager, and Graeme Stringer,
Recreation Ranger, at Forestry Commission Wales Coed y Brenin; the Public Rights of
Way Unit at Gwynedd Council in Dolgellau; and the National Trust in Ganllwyd.

CEFN COCH GOLD MINE

DESCRIPTION A fascinating 3-mile walk to a gold mine high on the slopes of Y Garn mountain, whose dramatic cliffs overlook Ganllwyd to the west. On the way back you walk along an old tramway to the ruined mine mill and barracks before descending to the valley floor to pass the splendid Plas Dolmelynllyn Hotel. Allow 3 hours.

START National Trust car park (free) east of the A470 in Ganllwyd. SH 728244.

DIRECTIONS *From Dolgellau:* Take the A470 towards Porthmadog and Blaenau Ffestiniog. Enter Coed y Brenin soon after Llanelltyd and pass the Ty'n y Groes Hotel on the left before reaching Ganllwyd. Immediately after the speed limit sign turn RIGHT into the National Trust car-park. *From Porthmadog:* Take the A487 (subsequently the A470) towards Dolgellau. Pass Trawsfynydd and Bronaber before entering Coed y Brenin. You'll see the entrance to the forest park visitor centre (on the left) before reaching Ganllwyd. Here look for a bus shelter on the left, followed by some houses, before you turn LEFT into the National Trust car park.

BUS SERVICE Buses X32 (Aberystwyth-Dolgellau-Porthmadog-Caernarvon/Bangor) and 35 (Dolgellau-Blaenau Ffestiniog) provide a regular service to Ganllwyd on Mondays to Saturdays.

1 Cross the A470, turn LEFT, cross a minor road and follow the footpath towards a white house. Turn RIGHT through a metal gate just before the house, and go uphill through a gateway towards a wooden gate and style. Go through/over and bear LEFT alongside a wall on the left. Follow the path uphill to a wooden gate. Cross the track beyond it and continue uphill past a marker. Ignore a path going off to the right as you follow the main track up to a marker post alongside a wall. Continue alongside the wall and turn LEFT through a gate to cross a wooden bridge.

2 Instead of going right at the marker beyond the bridge go HALF-RIGHT up a grassy track towards a ruined barn. Cross a tarmac road and walk uphill, going over a stile and then to the right of the ruined barn where there's another marker. After another stile and a metal gate, continue uphill, ignoring a gateway in the wall on your left. Soon bear HALF-RIGHT up to another marker. Here go HALF-LEFT and follow the winding path past two more markers to a wooden gate and stile. Go over the stile and up to the track beyond it. *The ruined building here was the explosives store for Cefn Coch gold mine. It was built here at a safe distance both from the mine workings (to the left) and the miners' barracks (to the right).*

3 Turn LEFT onto the track and follow it uphill to another ruin, behind which is a closed-off mine entrance (adit). *Cefn Coch was worked by the Welsh Gold Mining Company from 1862. A tramway to this point was constructed in 1864. The remains of it can be seen below the workings on the opposite side of the track to the ruin. The extent of the mine can be seen when you follow the track uphill to the RIGHT just after the ruin. The highest adit is about a quarter of a mile away and there are numerous fenced-off shafts and spoil-heaps. Please note that children should be carefully supervised in this area. From the highest point of the mine workings there is a magnificent view of Coed y Brenin with the peak of Rhobell Fawr towering above it to the east.*

4 Go back down to the low adit, pass it, then leave the track to join a raised tramway and path. This takes you above the explosives store, then down to some ruined mine buildings. Go LEFT behind the buildings to the end wall, then RIGHT downhill alongside it. Turn RIGHT again, walk along the front of the ruins and go HALF-LEFT to join the track below. *These ruined buildings are the site of the mine mill. Alongside the track to the right are the remains of the miners' barracks.* Go LEFT onto the track and follow it to a marker post. Turn RIGHT here and follow a path over a wooden bridge and through a gate. Go RIGHT onto a track. At a

junction, go HALF-RIGHT downhill alongside a wall. Ignore a track on the left and then
turn RIGHT at a tarmac road.

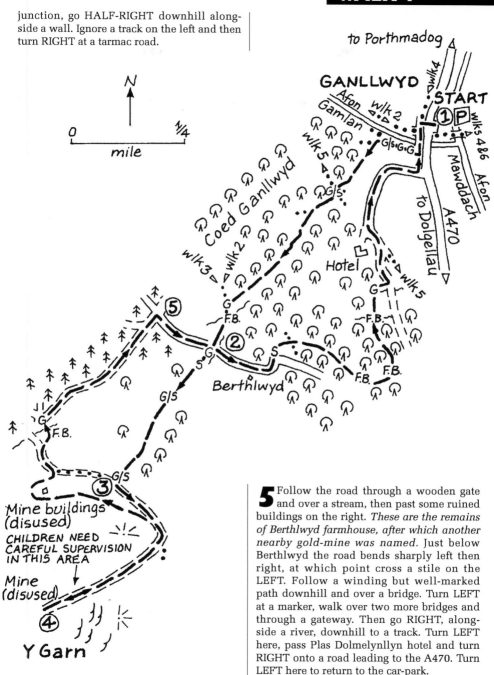

5 Follow the road through a wooden gate
and over a stream, then past some ruined
buildings on the right. *These are the remains
of Berthlwyd farmhouse, after which another
nearby gold-mine was named.* Just below
Berthlwyd the road bends sharply left then
right, at which point cross a stile on the
LEFT. Follow a winding but well-marked
path downhill and over a bridge. Turn LEFT
at a marker, walk over two more bridges and
through a gateway. Then go RIGHT, alongside a river, downhill to a track. Turn LEFT
here, pass Plas Dolmelynllyn hotel and turn
RIGHT onto a road leading to the A470. Turn
LEFT here to return to the car-park.

3

WALK 2

RHAEADR DU & AFON GAMLAN

This is a dramatic spot with wonderful views of the falls. The Gamlan flows from a wild area of moorland and bog below Y Lethr, the highest mountain in the Rhinog range to the west.

DESCRIPTION This 3½-mile walk takes you past the spectacular Rhaeadr Du (Black Waterfalls) and climbs to remote settlements high on Y Garn mountain from where there are fine views of Coed y Brenin. You then descend to the valley of the Afon Gamlan, cross the river on a bridge in the forest and follow its course back down to Ganllwyd. Allow 3 hours.

START National Trust car park (free) east of the A470 in Ganllwyd. SH 728244.

DIRECTIONS *From Dolgellau:* Take the A470 towards Porthmadog and Blaenau Ffestiniog. Enter Coed y Brenin soon after Llanelltyd and pass the Ty'n y Groes Hotel on the left before reaching Ganllwyd. Immediately after the speed limit sign turn RIGHT into the National Trust car-park. *From Porthmadog:* Take the A487 (subsequently the A470) towards Dolgellau. Pass Trawsfynydd and Bronaber before entering Coed y Brenin. You'll see the entrance to the forest park visitor centre on the left before reaching Ganllwyd. Here look for a bus shelter on the left, followed by some houses, before you turn LEFT into the National Trust car park.

BUS SERVICE Buses X32 (Aberystwyth-Dolgellau-Porthmadog-Caernarvon/Bangor) and 35 (Dolgellau-Blaenau Ffestiniog) provide a regular service to Ganllwyd on Mondays to Saturdays. .

1 Cross the A470, turn LEFT and pass Ganllwyd village hall. Go RIGHT onto the minor road beyond it and through a wooden gate. Continue uphill, ignoring a right-turn, and pass a marker on the left. Soon, when the road bears right, go uphill to a marker and turn LEFT. Walk downhill past another marker to cross a bridge over the Afon Gamlan. Go through the gate at the bridge end, then AHEAD to a marker and turn RIGHT. Follow the path over a stream and then uphill as it skirts the Rhaeadr Du. *Please take care! The path is often slippery and there are steep cliffs above the river.* The path levels off alongside the top of the falls.

2 Continue uphill on the path, bear LEFT at another marker and go up to a wall. Turn LEFT by the marker there, go over some wooden walkways and move closer to the wall before bearing RIGHT alongside it. Cross a stream, go LEFT at the next marker, then follow the path over a bridge alongside a stile to a kissing-gate. Go through and turn RIGHT at a marker to walk alongside a wall to a wooden gate. Go LEFT through this, across the bridge, turn RIGHT at a marker and walk uphill to a tarmac road. Turn RIGHT, following the road over a bridge and through a wooden gate. Soon turn LEFT onto a track going uphill. Then bear LEFT at a marker. *As you get higher you'll get your first views ahead of the magnificent cliffs of Y Garn. This mountain overlooks Ganllwyd and is an outlying peak of the Rhinog mountains.* Continue uphill to a junction.

3 Here, ignore a marker pointing left. Instead, go RIGHT, then immediately LEFT, onto a forestry track going uphill. Pass two yellow markers before reaching a wooden gate, followed by a cattle grid and second gate, at the forest edge. As indicated by a yellow marker, go through/over and LEFT at a junction near a barn before going uphill. *Over to the right is the farm of Gwndwn Isaf; soon you'll pass Gwndwn Uchaf ('Isaf' means 'lower' and 'uchaf' means 'upper'.)* Go through two gateways, past another cattle grid, and follow the track until you reach the left turn for Gwndwn Uchaf. *Pause here for a panoramic view of Coed y Brenin with the summit of Rhobell Fawr above it to the east.* Continue AHEAD at a yellow marker to follow a track downhill, through a metal gate, then to a forestry track.

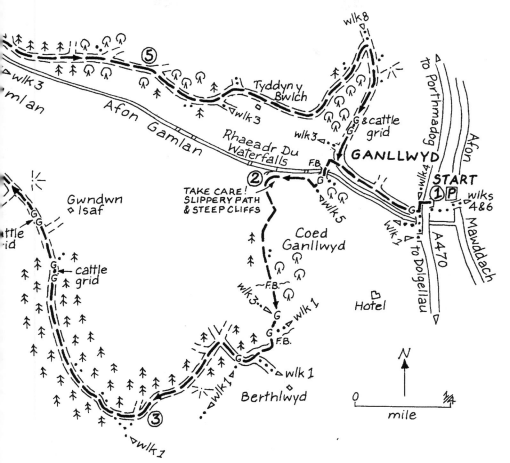

4 Turn RIGHT and follow the track downhill. *You are now back in the valley of the Afon Gamlan and will follow the river back to Ganllwyd. The Rhinog mountain ridge can be glimpsed at the head of the valley (to the left).* Quite soon, go LEFT at a junction and cross a bridge over the Gamlan. Immediately bear RIGHT and keep RIGHT to follow the track downhill alongside the river. Ignore a cycle trail, a path and then a forestry track, all on the left.

5 Before long, turn RIGHT at a junction and pass a sign saying 'Araf/Slow', before continuing downhill. Ignore a wooden gate on the right and pass Tyddyn y Bwlch house on the right. Follow the track, passing several markers, a path going right and a grass track on the left. Soon, at a junction below a communications mast, turn RIGHT by a marker. *Pause here for a good view over Ganllwyd and the Mawddach valley.* Descend to a wooden gate and cattle grid, followed by a metal gate. Go through and join the road back down to Ganllwyd.

WALK 3
AFON GAMLAN & GOETRE

DESCRIPTION Ganllwyd is famous for the dramatic Rhaeadr Du (Black Waterfalls) just above the village on the Afon Gamlan (see **Walks 2, 5** and **9**). On this 2½-mile walk you'll follow the course of the Gamlan as you walk up through Coed y Brenin to a bridge over the river. Having crossed it you then return to the village on the south of the river, gaining spectacular views over the forest before passing the old settlement of Goetre. Allow 2 hours.

START National Trust car park (free) east of the A470 in Ganllwyd. SH 728244.

DIRECTIONS *From Dolgellau:* Take the A470 towards Porthmadog and Blaenau Ffestiniog. Enter Coed y Brenin soon after Llanelltyd and pass the Ty'n y Groes Hotel on the left before reaching Ganllwyd. Immediately after the speed limit sign turn RIGHT into the National Trust car-park. *From Porthmadog:* Take the A487 (subsequently the A470) towards Dolgellau. Pass Trawsfynydd and Bronaber before entering Coed y Brenin. You'll see the entrance to the forest park visitor centre on the left before reaching Ganllwyd. Here look for a bus shelter on the left, followed by some houses, before you turn LEFT into the National Trust car park.

BUS SERVICE Buses X32 (Aberystwyth-Dolgellau-Porthmadog-Caernarvon/Bangor) and 35 (Dolgellau-Blaenau Ffestiniog) provide a regular service to Ganllwyd on Mondays to Saturdays.

1 Cross the A470, turn LEFT and pass the Ganllwyd village hall. Go RIGHT onto the minor road beyond it and through a wooden gate. Follow the road uphill, ignoring a right-turn, and pass a marker on the left. When the road bears right ignore a path going ahead and continue to where the tarmac ends. Turn LEFT here, going uphill on a stony track between banks to a wooden gate. Go through, following a path alongside a wall. Ignore a yellow marker indicating a path to the right and cross a slate bridge before walking uphill to go through anoth-

er wooden gate. Continue uphill between stone walls, ignoring gateways to the adjoining fields, and pass the settlement of Tyddyn y Bwlch before reaching another wooden gate.

2 Go through and turn LEFT onto the forestry track beyond. Walk uphill and soon go LEFT at a junction to join a wider forestry track which continues uphill. *As you gain height you'll hear the roar of the rapids on the Gamlan river below to the left.* High above you, also on the left, are the precipitous cliffs of Y Garn mountain. Ignore, on the right, a forestry track, then a yellow-marked path and a cycle track, before reaching a junction of tracks. Go LEFT here and keep LEFT at the junctions ahead to reach a bridge over the Afon Gamlan. *This is a beautiful area with wonderful views of the fast-flowing river. The Gamlan flows from a wild area of moorland and bog below Y Lethr, the highest mountain in the Rhinog range to the west of the bridge.*

3 Cross the bridge and bear LEFT at the junction of tracks beyond. Walk downhill and, before long, pass through a stand of trees before going through a gate into a clearing. *The next stretch of the walk provides wonderful views of Coed y Brenin and of Rhobell Fawr to the east of it. You can also see part of the distant Aran mountain ridge to the south-east.* Pass a track leading up to a house on the right before going through a wooden gate to reach the old settlement of Goetre.

4 Turn sharp LEFT just after the end wall of the house and go downhill on grass past a yellow marker and alongside a ruined barn to a wooden gate. Once through, follow a muddy path HALF-RIGHT past a telegraph pole and marker to a wall. Turn RIGHT at a marker near the wall and walk alongside it, ignoring an old gateway through it. Soon, cross a stream and pass another yellow marker before reaching a stile. Cross this, then go downhill, ignore a path at right-angles, and immediately go over another stile. Turn RIGHT then and over a wooden bridge to follow a path leading to a

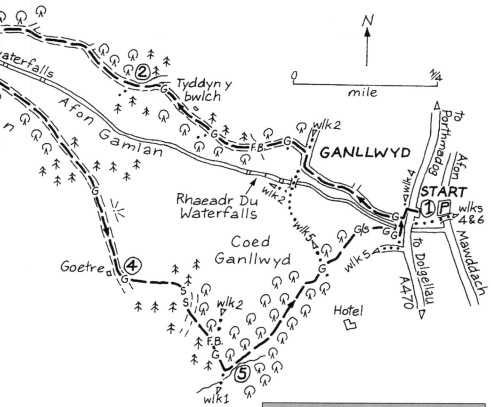

N

0 ———————— ¼
mile

Waterfalls

Afon Gamlan

Tyddyn y bwlch

wlk2

GANLLWYD

to Porthmadog

Afon Mawddach

START

wlks 4&6

Rhaeadr Du Waterfalls

wlk2

wlk5

to Dolgellau

A470

Coed Ganllwyd

wlk5

Goetre

Hotel

wlk2

F.B.

wlk1

green and white marker. Bear RIGHT here, cross a stream and then go through a wooden kissing-gate before arriving at a marker next to a wall ahead of you.

5 Turn LEFT here and follow a track going downhill away from the wall. Ignore a path going off to the left and continue down to a junction of tracks. Go through the wooden gate ahead of you and follow the track down alongside a wall to a stream. Cross this and make for the wooden gate and stile beyond it, after which continue downhill. Ignore two metal gates on the right and pass a white house on the right before reaching another metal gate next to a footpath sign. Go through, turn LEFT, cross a bridge and return to the car-park.

About the author, Michael Burnett

Michael is a musician who has written articles and presented radio programmes about Welsh traditional music. He is also the author of two other Kittiwake guides: the Rhinogs, and East of Snowdon.

Michael's links to Wales go back to his teenage years when he regularly stayed with friends near Maentwrog and to the 1970s when he lived with his wife, Paula, and their two young children at Blaen Myherin, a remote farmhouse above Devil's Bridge which has now, sadly, become a ruin. Today Michael and Paula share an old farmhouse near the northern Rhinog ridge.

WALK 4

AROUND GANLLWYD

DESCRIPTION A 1½-mile stroll which provides a good introduction the village of Ganllwyd and its locality. It offers views of the three rivers which converge on the village – the Gamlan, Mawddach and Eden – and takes you over a bridge which spans a spectacular gorge in the Mawddach valley. Allow 1 hour.

START National Trust car park (free) east of the A470 in Ganllwyd. SH 728244.

DIRECTIONS *From Dolgellau:* Take the A470 towards Porthmadog and Blaenau Ffestiniog. Enter Coed y Brenin soon after Llanelltyd and pass the Ty'n y Groes Hotel on the left before reaching Ganllwyd. Immediately after the speed limit sign turn RIGHT into the National Trust car park. *From Porthmadog:* Take the A487 (subsequently the A470) towards Dolgellau. Pass Trawsfynydd and Bronaber before entering Coed y Brenin. You'll see the entrance to the forest park visitor centre on the left before reaching Ganllwyd. Here look for a bus shelter on the left, followed by some houses, before you turn LEFT into the National Trust car park.

BUS SERVICE Buses X32 (Aberystwyth-Dolgellau-Porthmadog-Caernarvon/Bangor) and 35 (Dolgellau-Blaenau Ffestiniog) provide a regular service to/from Ganllwyd on Mondays to Saturdays.

1 Go down the path behind the car park alongside the Afon Gamlan (on the right). Cross the bridge over the Mawddach, go through a kissing-gate at its end, then follow a path through a second gate to a forestry track. Turn LEFT onto the track, passing two yellow markers and then a white marker. Soon, turn LEFT and cross Pont Cae'n y Coed footbridge. *Pause here for a wonderful view of the Mawddach gorge. During the floods in 2001 the Mawddach rose more than 10 metres and washed away the old stone bridge upstream at Abergeirw (see* **Walk 14**).

2 Bear LEFT at the bridge end and walk uphill to a tarmac road. Go LEFT along the road, ignoring a cycle track and forest track on the right. Soon the trees thin out and you can see parts of Ganllwyd including the impressive Plas Dolmelynllynn Hotel. Pass a BT substation and between gas pipeline markers at the sides of the road, then go LEFT onto a grassy path.

3 This takes you a short distance to the junction of the Eden and Mawddach rivers. *The remains of the crossing stones over the Afon Eden (on the right) can still be seen.* The bridge over the Afon Mawddach (to the left) is a pipeline crossing and inaccessible to walkers.

4 Return to the road, go LEFT, then LEFT again at a junction and across the bridge over the Eden. Walk uphill and go LEFT along the grass verge by the A470. Cross the road at the bus shelter and turn LEFT to join the footpath through Ganllwyd to the car park.

WALK 5

PLAS DOLMELYNLLYN & RHAEADR DU

DESCRIPTION This 1½-mile walk was inspired by a nature trail created in 2003 by the children of Ganllwyd primary school. A delightful pictorial map of the trail is mounted in the village bus shelter, and the school's headmistress, Mrs Kerry Wyn Parry, has given permission for the nature trail to be incorporated in this walk. It takes you round the attractive lake in the grounds of Plas Dolmelynllyn Hotel and then to the famous waterfalls on the Afon Gamlan. Allow 1½ hours.

START, DIRECTIONS & BUS SERVICE See **Walk 4**.

1 Cross the A470, turn LEFT, cross a minor road and walk towards a white house.

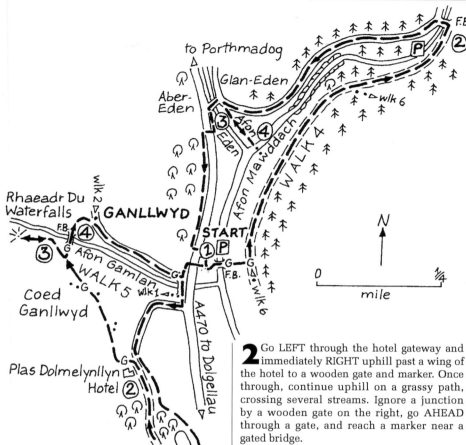

Pass the house and turn RIGHT onto the road to Plas Dolmelynllyn. Just before the hotel, at a junction alongside a stone arch, go LEFT downhill past houses on the left. Turn RIGHT just past some garages onto a path through the trees. At a junction of paths bear LEFT and follow the path around the Dolmelynllyn lake, ignoring a stile on the left before reaching another junction. Here go LEFT uphill to a track and marker. Turn RIGHT and walk over a bridge, and past the hotel, to the junction by the stone arch.

2 Go LEFT through the hotel gateway and immediately RIGHT uphill past a wing of the hotel to a wooden gate and marker. Once through, continue uphill on a grassy path, crossing several streams. Ignore a junction by a wooden gate on the right, go AHEAD through a gate, and reach a marker near a gated bridge.

3 Turn LEFT and follow the path over a stream and then uphill as it skirts the Rhaeadr Du (Black Waterfalls). *Please take care! The path is often slippery and there are steep cliffs above the river.* The path levels off alongside the top of the falls. *This is a dramatic spot with wonderful views of the falls on the Afon Gamlan. The Gamlan flows from a wild area of moorland and bog below Y Lethr, the highest mountain in the Rhinog range to the west.* Return downhill to the gated bridge.

4 Go LEFT across the bridge and uphill. At the second marker go RIGHT downhill to a tarmac road. Follow this back to the A470 and the car park.

9

FRIOG & PENRHOS ISAF

DESCRIPTION A 3½-mile walk which takes you to some interesting and isolated settlements high in Coed y Brenin above Ganllwyd. It offers some impressive views of the summit of Rhobell Fawr, to the east, and of the cliffs of Y Garn, which tower above the village to the west. Allow 3½ hours.

START National Trust car park (free) east of the A470 in Ganllwyd. SH 728244.

DIRECTIONS *From Dolgellau:* Take the A470 towards Porthmadog and Blaenau Ffestiniog. Enter Coed y Brenin soon after Llanelltyd and pass the Ty'n y Groes Hotel on the left before reaching Ganllwyd. Immediately after the speed limit sign turn RIGHT into the National Trust car park. *From Porthmadog:* Take the A487 (subsequently the A470) towards Dolgellau. Pass Trawsfynydd and Bronaber before entering Coed y Brenin. You'll see the entrance to the forest park visitor centre on the left before reaching Ganllwyd. Here look for a bus shelter on the left, followed by some houses, before you turn LEFT into the National Trust car park.

BUS SERVICE Buses X32 (Aberystwyth-Dolgellau-Porthmadog-Caernarvon/Bangor) and 35 (Dolgellau-Blaenau Ffestiniog) provide a regular service to/from Ganllwyd on Mondays to Saturdays.

1 Go down the path behind the car park alongside the Afon Gamlan (on the right) and onto the bridge over the Mawddach. This provides a spectacular viewpoint of the confluence of the two rivers. *The Rhaeadr Du (Black Waterfalls) on the Gamlan to the west are famous* (see **Walks 2**, **5** and **9**). Go through a metal kissing-gate at the end of the bridge, then follow a path through a second gate to a forestry track. Turn LEFT and follow the track past two yellow markers to a white marker on the right.

2 Go HALF-RIGHT here uphill on a path into the trees. Soon go over a stream

and reach a junction where you go RIGHT, then LEFT, then RIGHT. The path zig-zags uphill and arrives, after about ¼ mile, at a wooden post (on the left). Turn RIGHT here and go uphill initially alongside an old wall on the left. Eventually, when the path divides at a marker (blue arrows on white background), go LEFT uphill to meet a forestry track at a marker. Turn LEFT along the track to pass a wooden gate and reach the settlement of Friog. *This old house, with its outbuildings, dates back to the days when the area belonged to the Nannau estate. It is now almost completely surrounded by trees. Nannau house is near the village of Llanfachreth to the south-east of Friog.*

3 Continue on the track the short distance to a junction by a right-of-way sign. Go RIGHT past a wooden gate to where the track divides by a yellow marker. Go LEFT, ignore a path to the right, and walk to a marker on the right. Go RIGHT here onto a downhill path through the trees to another marker. Go AHEAD here, ignoring paths to right and left. Cross a stream and go uphill, past another marker, to a forestry track. Cross this, go AHEAD through trees to a track and turn RIGHT to reach Penrhos Isaf. *This isolated house is maintained by the Mountain Bothies Association for use by walkers (vehicular access is forbidden). The MBA (www.mountainbothiesassociation.org.uk) has seven bothies in Wales, including one at the foot of Arenig Fawr mountain eight miles to the north-east of Penrhos Isaf.*

4 Return to the point where you crossed the forestry track and go LEFT onto it. Walk uphill to a junction with a minor track on the left. *Pause here for a good view of the surrounding hills and valleys. The mountain summit dominating Coed y Brenin to the east is Rhobell Fawr.* The track goes downhill, past markers by a path on the left, to a cleared space adjoining a quarry. Look for a cycle track and forestry track on the right and a post with yellow markers to the left opposite a warning notice about the quarry.

5 Go LEFT at this post and downhill on a path past another marker. Soon bear

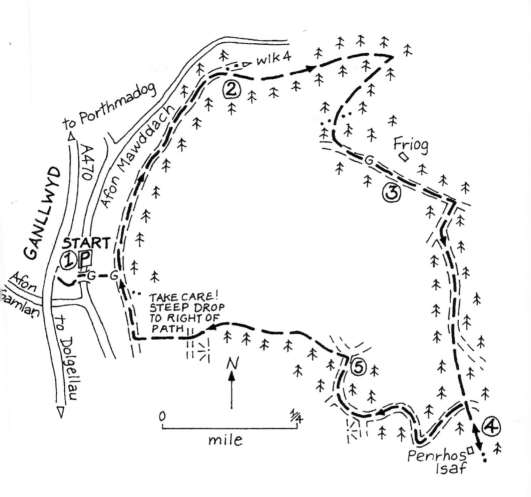

LEFT over a stream and pass a green marker and yellow marker after which bear RIGHT onto a path coming from the left. Soon the path goes down more steeply past a green marker and alongside the stream to emerge from the trees. *There's an excellent view over Ganllwyd to the cliffs of Y Garn mountain (see Walk 1) from here. Y Garn is an outlying peak of the Rhinog mountain range to the west. Prominent in the view below are the imposing buildings and carefully* *laid-out grounds of Plas Dolmelynllyn Hotel (see Walk 5).* Pass an electricity pole and go downhill very steeply. Take care at this point. There's a steep drop into a gully on the right. Soon cross a cycle track before continuing downhill to meet a forestry track by a white marker. Turn RIGHT onto the track, pass a house on the left, then go downhill LEFT to a metal kissing-gate. Return the way you came to the car park.

SARN HELEN & AFON EDEN

DESCRIPTION A fascinating 4½-mile walk which takes you along the route of a Roman road to a medieval smelting works high in Coed y Brenin. Magnificent views of the Rhinog mountains follow before you descend to the River Eden whose waters are home to freshwater pearl mussel, Atlantic salmon, water voles and otters. On the return you pass settlements high on the northern edge of the forest before crossing the Eden on the old stone bridge at Dolgefeiliau. Allow 4 hours.

START Coed y Brenin Forest Park Visitor Centre car park (fee payable). SH 725268.

DIRECTIONS *From Dolgellau:* Take the A470 towards Porthmadog and Blaenau Ffestiniog. Enter Coed y Brenin soon after Llanelltyd and pass the Ty'n y Groes Hotel on the left before going through Ganllwyd. A mile or so after the village turn RIGHT at the sign and drive the short distance to the Coed y Brenin Visitor Centre. *From Porthmadog:* Take the A487 (subsequently the A470) towards Dolgellau. Pass Trawsfynydd and Bronaber before entering Coed y Brenin. After a long, straight descent turn LEFT at the sign and drive the short distance to the Coed y Brenin Visitor Centre.

BUS SERVICE Buses X32 (Aberystwyth-Dolgellau-Porthmadog-Caernarvon/Bangor) and 35 (Dolgellau-Blaenau Ffestiniog) provide a regular service to/from the locality on Mondays to Saturdays. The X32 will stop on the A470 near the entrance to the Visitor Centre; most 35 buses call at the bus-stop at the Centre itself. *The Visitor Centre café offers a 10% reduction on production of an Arriva bus ticket.*

I Walk towards the visitor centre from the car park and bear LEFT on the road above it. Then go RIGHT onto a path signposted for several walks including 'Sarn Helen'. Immediately go LEFT onto another path which winds uphill to a forestry track. Turn RIGHT here and follow the track past a yellow marker uphill to a viewpoint. *From*

here there is a splendid view of Cadair Idris to the south-west. Go through a metal gate and LEFT uphill. Soon bear LEFT at a junction and continue on a track going north. *You are now following the course of the Roman road Sarn Helen from Tomen y Mur, near Trawsfynydd, to Brithdir, near Dolgellau. The original road from Trawsfynydd to Dolgellau also came this way.*

2 Pass an area where the track has been widened and go uphill. Soon, when the track divides, bear LEFT and continue uphill the short distance to an old milestone on the right. *The milestone is above the track just inside the trees and relates to the old Trawsfynydd-Dolgellau road. The latter (shown as Dolgelley) is 7 miles distant.* Soon after the milestone the track reaches the site of the Llwyn Du bloomery on the right. *This was a medieval iron working settlement, built here because charcoal was readily available from the nearby forest. The site was initially excavated in 1997 and partly reconstructed in 2001. Look out for the excavated remains of two furnaces.*

3 Return to the track and turn RIGHT uphill. Soon the track levels off and you pass a walled field on the left before reaching a junction. *Just before this there is a magnificent view of the Rhinog mountains to the left. The main peaks are (from right to left) Rhinog Fawr, Rhinog Fach and Y Lethr.* At the junction go LEFT (Sarn Helen goes right here) down a tarmac road, passing Bwlch y Ffordd house on the left. Follow the road, eventually crossing a stream before reaching a footpath sign on the left. Go LEFT here and downhill, crossing a forestry track next to a marker before reaching the main A470 road. Taking great care, cross this and continue along the minor road opposite. Bear RIGHT past Gelli Goch house and go downhill until you see the Afon Eden. Bear RIGHT when the road divides and cross the bridge.

4 Follow the road to another bridge and metal gate. Immediately after the gate go LEFT and cross a track to a stile. After, continue ahead making for a large tree. Pass this and bear RIGHT towards the wall, going

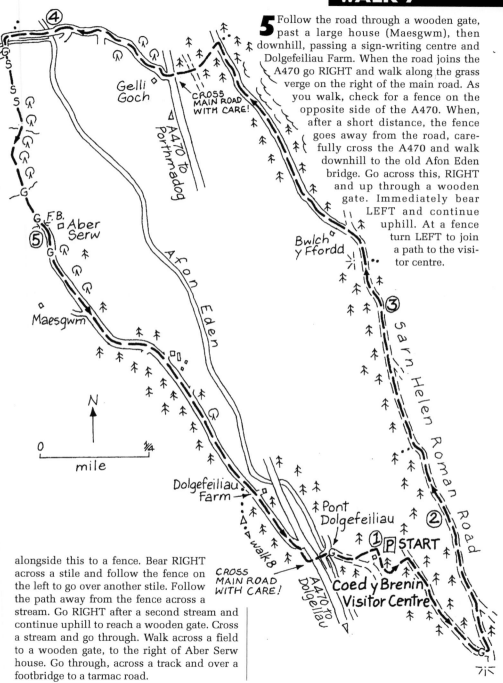

5 Follow the road through a wooden gate, past a large house (Maesgwm), then downhill, passing a sign-writing centre and Dolgefeiliau Farm. When the road joins the A470 go RIGHT and walk along the grass verge on the right of the main road. As you walk, check for a fence on the opposite side of the A470. When, after a short distance, the fence goes away from the road, carefully cross the A470 and walk downhill to the old Afon Eden bridge. Go across this, RIGHT and up through a wooden gate. Immediately bear LEFT and continue uphill. At a fence turn LEFT to join a path to the visitor centre.

Map labels:
- Gelli Goch
- CROSS MAIN ROAD WITH CARE!
- A470 to Porthmadog
- Afon Eden
- F.B.
- Aber Serw
- Maesgwm
- Bwlch y Ffordd
- Sarn Helen Roman Road
- N
- 0 ¼ mile
- Dolgefeiliau Farm
- walk 8
- Pont Dolgefeiliau
- CROSS MAIN ROAD WITH CARE!
- A470 to Dolgellau
- P START
- Coed y Brenin Visitor Centre

alongside this to a fence. Bear RIGHT across a stile and follow the fence on the left to go over another stile. Follow the path away from the fence across a stream. Go RIGHT after a second stream and continue uphill to reach a wooden gate. Cross a stream and go through. Walk across a field to a wooden gate, to the right of Aber Serw house. Go through, across a track and over a footbridge to a tarmac road.

TYDDYN Y BWLCH & AFON GAMLAN

DESCRIPTION This 5½-mile walk explores the forest to the west of the Afon Eden. It takes you high above the village of Ganllwyd and, after passing the remote settlement of Tyddyn y Bwlch, to a bridge over the fast-flowing Afon Gamlan. You then visit two viewpoints in Coed y Brenin from where, thanks to recent forest clearances, there are magnificent views of the surrounding area. Allow 4½ hours.

START Coed y Brenin Forest Park Visitor Centre car park (fee payable). SH 725268.

DIRECTIONS *From Dolgellau:* Take the A470 towards Porthmadog and Blaenau Ffestiniog. Enter Coed y Brenin soon after Llanelltyd and pass the Ty'n y Groes Hotel on the left before going through Ganllwyd. A mile or so after the village turn RIGHT at the sign and drive the short distance to the Coed y Brenin Visitor Centre. *From Porthmadog:* Take the A487 (subsequently the A470) towards Dolgellau. Pass Trawsfynydd and Bronaber before entering Coed y Brenin. After a long, straight descent turn LEFT at the sign and drive the short distance to the Coed y Brenin Visitor Centre.

BUS SERVICE Buses X32 (Aberystwyth-Dolgellau-Porthmadog-Caernarvon/Bangor) and 35 (Dolgellau-Blaenau Ffestiniog) provide a regular service to/from the locality on Mondays to Saturdays. The X32 will stop on the A470 near the entrance to the Visitor Centre; most 35 buses call at the bus-stop at the Centre itself. *The Visitor Centre café offers a 10% reduction on production of an Arriva bus ticket.*

I Go downhill on the right of the visitor centre to a track. Turn RIGHT downhill past a wooden gate and then go through a second gate to cross the old bridge over the Afon Eden. Continue AHEAD at the bridge end and walk uphill to the A470 road. Carefully cross the main road, then turn RIGHT and walk along the grass verge on the left of the A470. After a short distance, turn LEFT onto a minor road. Follow this past Dolgefeiliau Farm, then turn LEFT onto a forestry track going uphill by a sign banning cars. Go through a wooden gate then continue on the track for a mile or so, ignoring cycle tracks left and right, to a junction. Go LEFT here and walk to a second junction at a blue marker. Go LEFT downhill on a narrower track to a junction of three tracks next to a communications mast. *This point provides a wonderful view over the Mawddach valley (to the left) and Ganllwyd. The village is famous for the spectacular Rhaeadr Du waterfalls on the Afon Gamlan* (see **Walks 2**, **5** and **9**).

2 Take the middle track (indicated with a yellow marker) and walk uphill. Soon pass another yellow marker where a path goes left, and then a white marker, before reaching Tyddyn y Bwlch house on the left. Pass a yellow marker here and continue uphill ignoring a gate on the left. Soon go LEFT at a junction to join a wider forestry road which continues uphill. *As you gain height you'll hear the roar of the rapids on the Gamlan river below to the left. Above the river, also on the left, are the precipitous cliffs of Y Garn mountain.* Ignore, on the right, a forestry track, a yellow-marked path and a cycle track, before reaching a junction of tracks. Go LEFT here and keep LEFT at the junctions ahead to reach a bridge over the Afon Gamlan. *The Gamlan flows from a wild area of moorland and bog below Y Lethr, the highest mountain in the Rhinog range to the west of the bridge.*

3 Return, for a short distance, the way you came. Ignore the first track on the left immediately after the bridge but take the second track, going LEFT uphill away from the junction you passed earlier. Go past a wooden gate and markers to left and right as you walk alongside cleared forest on the right. Pass 'Tarw' cycle track signs to left and right, then go RIGHT at a junction above the cleared forest. *Pause as you climb and look behind to see Diffwys, the southernmost peak of the Rhinog ridge, in the distance.* Pass two markers on the right before the track goes through a stand of trees and descends.

Follow it for ½ mile or so to a junction.

4 Turn RIGHT, continuing downhill. *The next stretch of track provides panoramic views. You can see over Coed y Brenin to Rhobell Fawr which dominates the scene to the south-east. As you descend you'll see the forest Visitor Centre far below in the Eden Valley.* Soon pass a turning circle and ignore a track going to the right. At the next junction continue AHEAD as indicated by a blue marker. Go sharp LEFT at the junction after and follow this track a mile or so down to a tarmac road. Turn RIGHT and retrace your steps to the forest Visitor Centre.

wlk7 | Dolgefeiliau Farm

START
①P Coed y Brenin Visitor Centre

wlk7

CROSS MAIN ROAD WITH CARE!

Afon Eden

④

A470 to Porthmadog

N

0 _____ ¼
mile

A470 to Dolgellau

Afon Eden

②

Aber Eden

③

wlk 2

Afon Gamlan

waterfalls

Tyddyn y Bwlch

wlk 2

GANLLWYD

P

(start wlks 1-6)

15

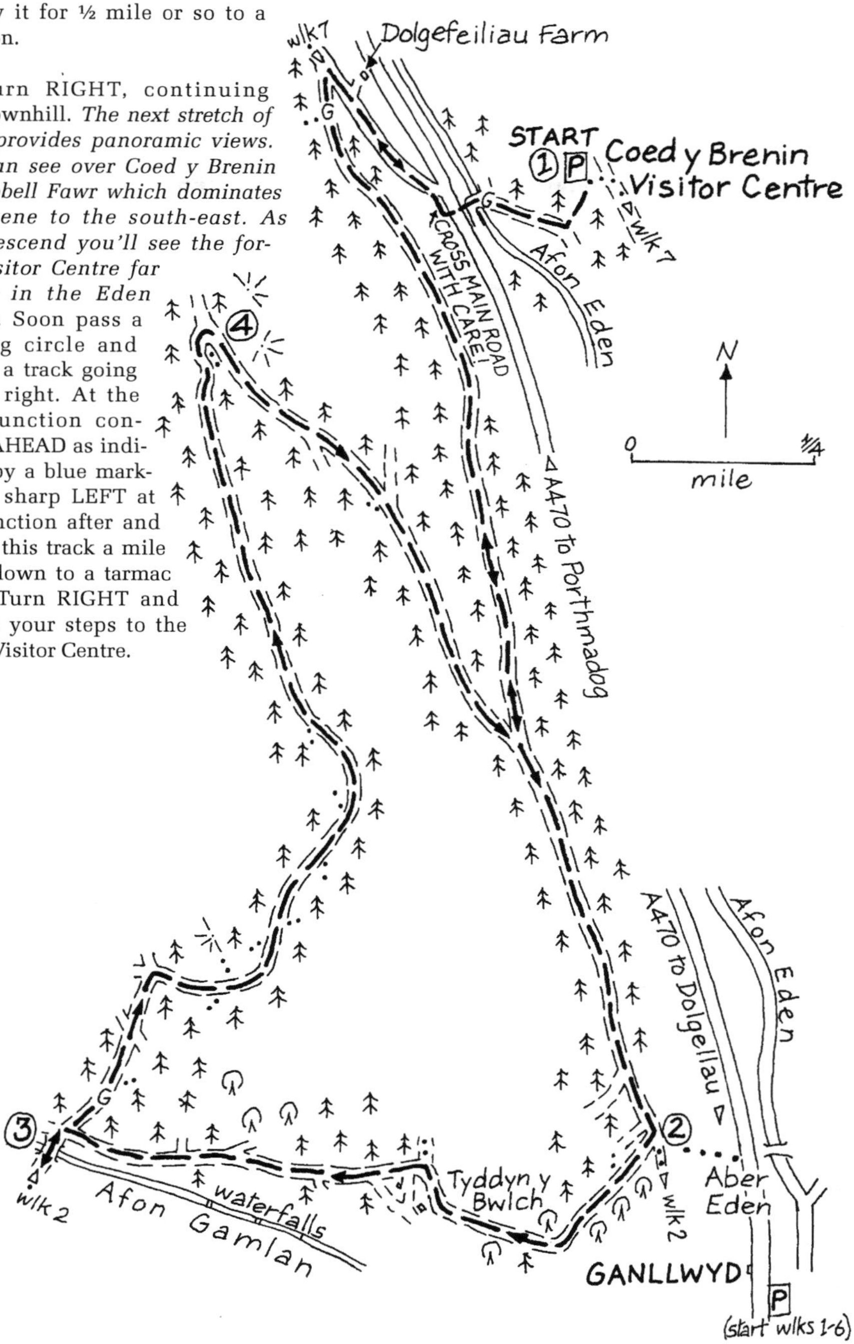

WALK 9

PONT CAE'N Y COED & RHAEADR DU

DESCRIPTION This varied 5½-mile walk takes you to a spectacular viewpoint in Coed y Brenin before descending to cross the fast-flowing Afon Mawddach. A second footbridge then takes you across the Mawddach again before you climb to the magnificent waterfalls of Rhaeadr Du (Black Waterfalls) near the village of Ganllwyd. On the return you walk through the forest above the Afon Eden, the river which flows through Coed y Brenin from north to south. Allow 4½ hours.

START Coed y Brenin forest park visitor centre car park (fee payable). SH 725268.

DIRECTIONS *From Dolgellau:* Take the A470 towards Porthmadog and Blaenau Ffestiniog. Enter Coed y Brenin soon after Llanelltyd and pass the Ty'n y Groes Hotel on the left before going through Ganllwyd. A mile or so after the village turn RIGHT at the sign and drive the short distance to the Coed y Brenin Visitor Centre. *From Porthmadog:* Take the A487 (subsequently the A470) towards Dolgellau. Pass Trawsfynydd and Bronaber before entering Coed y Brenin. After a long, straight descent turn LEFT at the sign and drive the short distance to the Coed y Brenin Visitor Centre.

BUS SERVICE Buses X32 (Aberystwyth-Dolgellau-Porthmadog-Caernarvon/Bangor) and 35 (Dolgellau-Blaenau Ffestiniog) provide a regular service to/from the locality on Mondays to Saturdays. The X32 will stop on the A470 near the entrance to the Visitor Centre; most 35 buses call at the bus-stop at the centre itself. *The Visitor Centre café offers a 10% reduction on production of an Arriva bus ticket.*

1 Walk towards the visitor centre from the car park and bear LEFT on the road above it. Then go RIGHT onto a path signposted for several walks including 'Cefndeuddwr Trail'. This climbs to meet a forestry track. Turn RIGHT here and walk the short distance to a viewpoint. Pass through a metal gateway, cross a forestry track and go AHEAD, uphill on a marked path. *The ancient farm of Cefndeuddwr can be seen over the fields to the right from here.* Follow the path a short distance to a forestry track and turn RIGHT at a marker to follow the track to a junction where several trails go left. Turn RIGHT here, passing a white post on the left, and walk downhill to another junction. Ignore the gate on the right and continue AHEAD. The track takes you behind Cefndeuddwr and eventually reaches a cleared space by a sharp bend to the left. *Pause here for a spectacular view over the forest to the summit of Rhobell Fawr.*

2 Follow the track round to the LEFT and downhill for a short distance to a white marker. Turn RIGHT here and follow a path downhill. Eventually go RIGHT onto a tarmac road, and then immediately LEFT to cross Pont Cae'n y Coed footbridge. *Pause here for a wonderful view of the Mawddach gorge.* Go RIGHT after the bridge and follow a forestry track past white and yellow markers to a ruined barn on the right. Soon go RIGHT, through two kissing-gates and over the Mawddach again. Go uphill to Ganllwyd car park and make for the noticeboard on the left. Walk past this, then turn LEFT by a wall, and RIGHT through a wooden gate to the A470 road.

3 Cross the A470, turn LEFT and pass Ganllwyd village hall. Go RIGHT onto the minor road beyond it and through a wooden gate. Continue uphill, ignoring a right-turn, and pass a marker on the left. Soon, when the road bears right, go uphill to a marker and turn LEFT. Walk downhill past another marker to cross a bridge over the Afon Gamlan. Go through the gate at the bridge end, then AHEAD to a marker and turn RIGHT. Follow the path over a stream and uphill by the Rhaeadr Du. *Please take care! The path is often slippery and there are steep cliffs above the river.* The path levels off alongside the top of the falls. *This is a dramatic spot with wonderful views of the falls.*

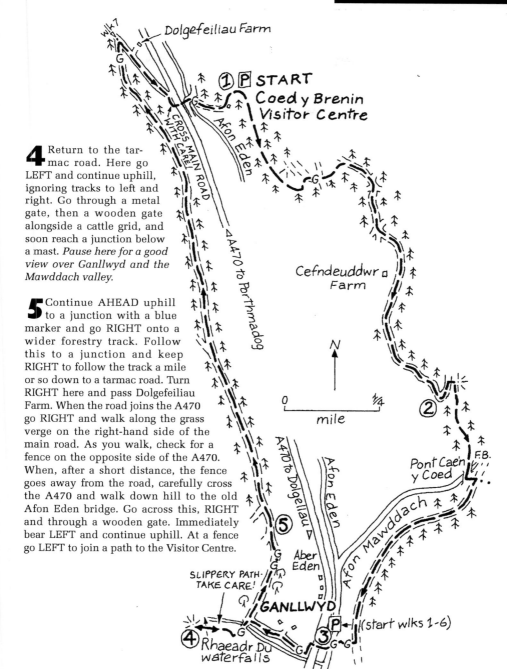

Dolgefeiliau Farm

① P **START**
Coed y Brenin
Visitor Centre

4 Return to the tarmac road. Here go LEFT and continue uphill, ignoring tracks to left and right. Go through a metal gate, then a wooden gate alongside a cattle grid, and soon reach a junction below a mast. *Pause here for a good view over Ganllwyd and the Mawddach valley.*

5 Continue AHEAD uphill to a junction with a blue marker and go RIGHT onto a wider forestry track. Follow this to a junction and keep RIGHT to follow the track a mile or so down to a tarmac road. Turn RIGHT here and pass Dolgefeiliau Farm. When the road joins the A470 go RIGHT and walk along the grass verge on the right-hand side of the main road. As you walk, check for a fence on the opposite side of the A470. When, after a short distance, the fence goes away from the road, carefully cross the A470 and walk down hill to the old Afon Eden bridge. Go across this, RIGHT and through a wooden gate. Immediately bear LEFT and continue uphill. At a fence go LEFT to join a path to the Visitor Centre.

Afon Eden

CROSS MAIN ROAD WITH CARE!

A470 to Porthmadog

Cefndeuddwr □ Farm

N

0   ¼
  mile

②

A470 to Dolgellau

Afon Eden

Pont Caeh
y Coed   F.B.

Afon Mawddach

⑤

Aber
Eden

SLIPPERY PATH·
TAKE CARE!

GANLLWYD

P ←(start wlks 1-6)

④ Rhaeadr Du
waterfalls   ③

17

WALK 10

PISTYLL CAIN & TYDDYN GLWADYS

DESCRIPTION A 4½-mile walk on which you visit two impressive waterfalls deep in the heart of Coed y Brenin. You then climb up into the forest alongside the fast-flowing Afon Gain before leaving the river to reach the ancient settlement of Tyddyn Gwladys. You then walk along a high track which offers wonderful views over the Mawddach valley. Allow 3½ hours.

START Coed y Brenin Forest Park Visitor Centre car park (fee payable). SH 725268.

DIRECTIONS *From Dolgellau:* Take the A470 towards Porthmadog and Blaenau Ffestiniog. Enter Coed y Brenin soon after Llanelltyd and pass the Ty'n y Groes Hotel on the left before going through Ganllwyd. A mile or so after the village turn RIGHT at the sign and drive the short distance to the Coed y Brenin Visitor Centre. *From Porthmadog:* Take the A487 (subsequently the A470) towards Dolgellau. Pass Trawsfynydd and Bronaber before entering Coed y Brenin. After a long, straight descent turn LEFT at the sign and drive the short distance to the Coed y Brenin Visitor Centre.

BUS SERVICE Buses X32 (Aberystwyth-Dolgellau-Porthmadog-Caernarvon/Bangor) and 35 (Dolgellau-Blaenau Ffestiniog) provide a regular service to/from the locality on Mondays to Saturdays. The X32 will stop on the A470 near the entrance to the Visitor Centre; most 35 buses call at the bus-stop at the Centre itself. *The visitor centre café offers a 10% reduction on production of an Arriva bus ticket.*

I Walk towards the visitor centre from the car park and bear LEFT on the road above it. Then go RIGHT onto a path signposted for several walks including 'Cefndeuddwr Trail'. This climbs to meet a forestry track. Turn RIGHT here and walk the short distance to a viewpoint. Pass through a metal gateway, cross a forestry track and go AHEAD, uphill on a marked path. *The ancient farm of*

Cefndeuddwr can be seen over the fields to the right from here. Cefndeuddr means 'the ridge between two waters'. The 'waters' are, of course, Afon Mawddach, whose famous falls you will visit later on the walk, and Afon Eden (see **Walk 11**). Follow this path a short distance to a forestry track and turn RIGHT at a marker to follow the track to a junction where several trails go left. Turn RIGHT here, passing a white post on the left, and go downhill to another junction.

2 Ignore the gate on the right and take the grassy track on the LEFT, following it to a clearing where you should take a path, with white marker, on the LEFT. This goes through the trees and passes another white marker before crossing mine workings alongside a wall. Continue into the trees beyond, go through a wall and follow the path uphill and gradually away from the wall. Soon reach a white marker, after which descend to another marker and turn RIGHT. Go downhill, passing a series of markers as the path winds round before reaching a grassy track by a white marker (no 29).

3 Turn RIGHT here, go downhill for a short distance then take a marked path on the LEFT. At a forestry track go LEFT and walk the short distance to a bridge over the Afon Gain. *Go LEFT at the end of the bridge for a good view of the Pistyll Cain waterfalls.* Then continue on the track, bearing LEFT at a junction and going uphill to a good viewpoint for the Rhaeadr Mawddach falls and, alongside them, part of the Gwynfynydd gold mine. *This area was the scene of the first Welsh gold rush during the early 1860s. Gold was discovered at Gwynfyndd in 1863. However, finds were subsequently sporadic until, in 1887, a lode containing good quality gold was found on the hillside above the falls. A second gold rush then led to over 25 mines becoming operational locally.* Retrace your steps over the Afon Gain to white marker no 29.

4 Continue past the marker, walking uphill on the track above the Afon Gain. After a time pass a wooden gate, noting the bridge below right. Turn LEFT onto a wide forestry

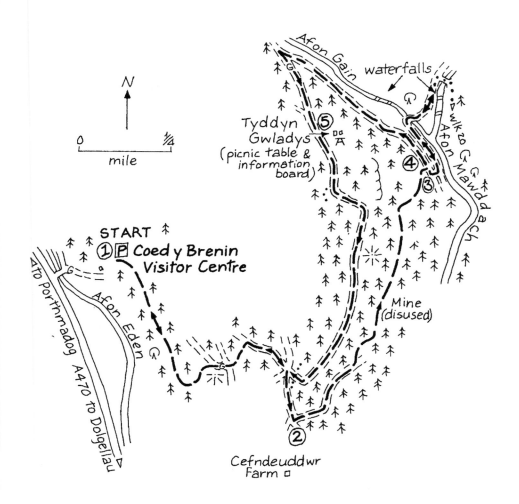

track, passing a white marker and a gate, as you go uphill. Ignore two paths on the left, and one on the right with a yellow marker, before arriving at the site of the old settlement of Tyddyn Gwladys. *Information on the settlement and on local wildlife is provided here, together with a picnic table.*

5 Continue on the track, ignoring a path on the right, and passing a white marker on the left and, later, a yellow marker on the right. *As you walk you will enjoy a magnificent panorama of the Mawddach valley. Later there are good views of the ridge of Cadair Idris to the south and the peak of Y Garn (one of the Rhinog mountain range) to the west.* At a junction continue AHEAD on the track you followed earlier and, soon, turn LEFT at a marker onto a path going downhill. Retrace your steps from here to the Forest Visitor Centre.

PONT CAE'N Y COED & CEFNDEUDDWR

DESCRIPTION This 4½-mile walk takes you through the dramatic Eden and Mawddach valleys before climbing to a spectacular viewpoint in Coed y Brenin. From here you continue high in the forest to another viewpoint near the old settlement of Cefndeuddwr before descending once more to the Eden valley. Allow 3½ hours.

START Coed y Brenin Visitor Centre car-park (fee payable). SH 725268.

DIRECTIONS *From Dolgellau:* Take the A470 towards Porthmadog and Blaenau Ffestiniog. Enter Coed y Brenin soon after Llanelltyd and pass the Ty'n y Groes Hotel on the left before going through Ganllwyd. A mile or so after the village turn RIGHT at the sign and drive the short distance to the Coed y Brenin Forest Park Visitor Centre. *From Porthmadog:* Take the A487 (subsequently the A470) towards Dolgellau. Pass Trawsfynydd and Bronaber before entering Coed y Brenin. After a long, straight descent turn LEFT at the sign and drive the short distance to the Coed y Brenin Forest Park Visitor Centre.

BUS SERVICE Buses X32 (Aberystwyth-Dolgellau-Porthmadog-Caernarvon/Bangor) and 35 (Dolgellau-Blaenau Ffestiniog) provide a regular service to/from the locality on Mondays to Saturdays. The X32 will stop on the A470 near the entrance to the Visitor Centre; most 35 buses call at the bus-stop at the Centre itself. *The Visitor Centre café offers a 10% reduction on production of an Arriva bus ticket.*

1 Walk towards the Visitor Centre from the car-park and go downhill to the RIGHT of the centre. At the first junction go LEFT onto a forestry track, passing a white marker on the right. Follow the track downhill, ignoring a path to the right and cycle track going left. *The river to your right is the Afon Eden, whose waters are protected as a Site of Special Scientific Interest. The river flows* from a large area of moorland below the Rhinog mountain ridge to the north. Its head waters contain the last breeding population of freshwater pearl mussels in Wales, and are home to water voles and otters. Soon the track reaches the floor of the valley where there are fields to the right. Pass a wooden gate, then a metal gate and ruined barn on the right, before going uphill to reach a tarmac road. Turn RIGHT onto the road, ignore a grass track going left then take a forestry track (marked cycle route 82) on the LEFT. Follow this track, which takes you from the Eden valley to the Mawddach valley, and eventually descends to another tarmac road. Ignore a path going ahead here but go LEFT onto this road. Ignore a cycle track on the left then go RIGHT downhill to reach Pont Cae'n y Coed footbridge over the Afon Mawddach. *Pause here for a wonderful view of the Mawddach gorge. During the floods in 2001 the river rose more than 10 metres and washed away the old stone bridge upstream at Abergeirw (see* **Walk 14***).*

2 Turn LEFT onto the track beyond the bridge and follow it uphill alongside the river. Bear LEFT at a junction and pass a wooden gate with a yellow marker. Enter a section of cleared forest (on the right) and pass a marker on the left. *The Afon Mawddach is confined in a narrow gorge below you to the left and there are many dramatic rapids and waterfalls.* Soon the track enters the forest again and, before long, you'll see a wooden footbridge over the river. Go LEFT downhill near a wooden seat to cross the bridge.

3 Walk uphill away from the bridge to the RIGHT on a gravel path. Go LEFT when this comes close to a tarmac road, then RIGHT onto the road. Take the next track on the LEFT at a white marker (post 28) and walk uphill past a metal gate. The track bends sharp left, passes twice under power lines and before long emerges from the forest. Pass a white marker and path on the left before arriving at a point where the track bends sharply right. *You have now reached one of the most spectacular viewpoints in Coed y Brenin. Below you is the Mawddach*

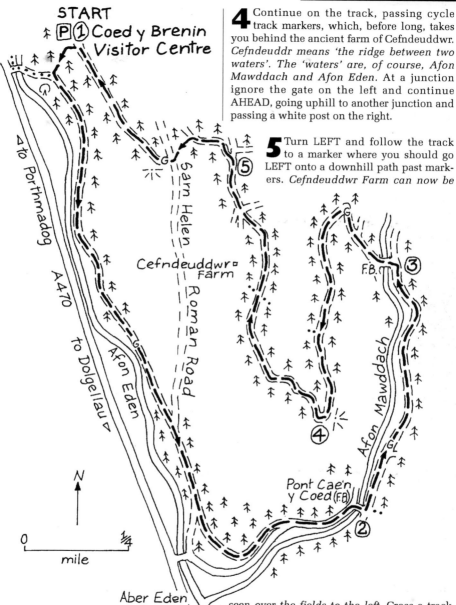

START
P① Coed y Brenin
Visitor Centre

to Porthmadog A470 to Dolgellau ▷

Afon Eden

Sarn Helen

Cefndeuddwr Farm

Roman Road

⑤

③

F.B.

④

GL

Afon Mawddach

Pont Cae'n y Coed (F.B)

②

N

0   ¼
      mile

Aber Eden

4 Continue on the track, passing cycle track markers, which, before long, takes you behind the ancient farm of Cefndeuddwr. *Cefndeuddr means 'the ridge between two waters'. The 'waters' are, of course, Afon Mawddach and Afon Eden.* At a junction ignore the gate on the left and continue AHEAD, going uphill to another junction and passing a white post on the right.

5 Turn LEFT and follow the track to a marker where you should go LEFT onto a downhill path past markers. *Cefndeuddwr Farm can now be*

valley and, to the south-east, you can see the summit of Rhobell Fawr high above the forest. Further away, to the south-west, is Cadair Idris above Dolgellau.

seen over the fields to the left. Cross a track and go through a metal gateway to a second viewpoint. After this, go LEFT onto a downhill forestry path which eventually joins a tarmac road. Turn LEFT to reach the Visitor Centre.

WALK 12

GWYNFYNYDD GOLD MINE

DESCRIPTION An exciting 2-mile walk which provides magnificent views of Coed y Brenin and of the valley of the Afon Mawddach. On the way you follow a path which winds its way down to the valley above a deep gorge in the river's course. Then you join a track which takes you through the workings of one of the area's best known gold mines. Allow 2 hours.

START Parking space above the Afon Mawddach near Bedd y Coedwr Farm. SH 736285.

DIRECTIONS *From Dolgellau:* Take the A470 towards Porthmadog and Blaenau Ffestiniog. Enter Coed y Brenin soon after Llanelltyd and pass the Ty'n y Groes Hotel on the left before going through Ganllwyd. Soon after the village pass the entrance to the Coed y Brenin Visitor Centre on the right and, after another two miles, turn RIGHT onto a minor road at Bronaber. Follow this road (signposted Llanuwchllyn/Abergeirw) through Trawsfynydd Holiday Village, ignoring a right turn for the Rhiwgoch pub. Bear RIGHT just past Penystryd Farm, cross a cattle-grid and then immediately turn RIGHT onto a road where there's a dead-end sign. Pass Penystryd chapel and go downhill to bridge the Afon Gain before entering Coed y Brenin. Continue uphill through the forest, passing a right turn signposted for cycle track 8 and then, also on the right, the track going to Gwynfynnyd Farm. Pass open fields, and then a track descending, on the right. Park soon after this in a clearing in the trees on the LEFT.
From Porthmadog: Take the A487 (subsequently the A470) towards Dolgellau. Pass Trawsfynydd and, after two miles, turn LEFT onto a minor road at Bronaber. Follow this road (signposted Llanuwchllyn/Abergeirw) through Trawsfynydd Holiday Village, ignoring a right turn for the Rhiwgoch pub. Bear RIGHT just past Penystryd Farm, cross a cattle-grid and then immediately turn RIGHT onto a road where there's a dead-end sign. Pass Penystryd chapel and go downhill to bridge the Afon Gain before entering Coed

y Brenin. Continue uphill through the forest, passing a right turn signposted for cycle track 8 and then, also on the right, the track going to Gwynfynydd Farm. Pass open fields, and then a track descending on the right. Park soon after this in a clearing in the trees on the LEFT.

1 Go LEFT and steeply downhill on the road. *There are magnificent views from here over the Mawddach valley and Coed y Brenin to Cadair Idris. You can also see the Rhinog mountains to the west and the summit of Rhobell Fawr to the south-east.* Soon, just before the gateway to Bedd y Coedwr Farm turn RIGHT at a footpath sign and follow a path downhill on the right of a stream and boundary wall.

2 Continue as the path bears to the right away from the stream and, soon, enter an area which has been identified as a Site of Special Scientific Interest. *Coed y Brenin has several such sites, the objective of which is to help preserve unique features of the landscape including, here, mosses, lichens and liverworts.* The path continues downill to a fenced-off mine entrance, with a warning notice, on the left. *This is a trial level belonging to the old Bedd y Coedwr gold mine.*

3 Bear RIGHT as the path descends towards the Mawddach river, winding its way above other Bedd y Coedwr workings (surrounded by wooden fencing) before reaching a rickety stile marked with a blue-painted wooden bar. Follow the path down to a metal-barred mine entrance on the right. A track begins here: follow it down to the river and, after a short distance, some of the Gwynfynydd mine buildings. *Please keep away from the track edge above the river as you walk to the mine: it is unstable and there is a steep drop. Also do NOT enter the mine buildings – THEY ARE DANGEROUS. This area was the scene of the first Welsh gold rush during the early 1860s. Gold was discovered at Gwynfyndd in 1863. However, finds were subsequently sporadic until, in 1887, a lode containing good quality gold was found on the hillside above you. A second gold rush then led to over 25 mines becoming operational locally.* Walk past the

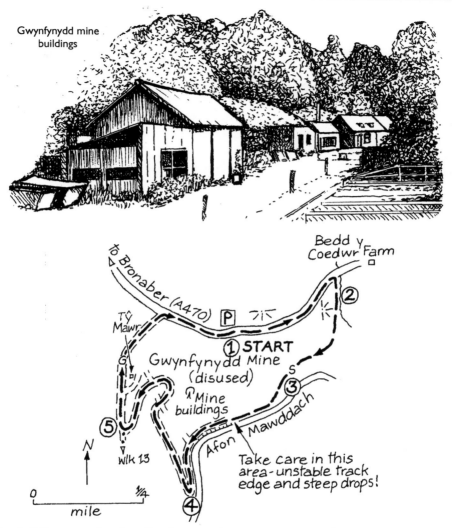

Gwynfynydd mine buildings

mine buildings, crossing the rails of a tram-way and passing a sluice on the left.

4 Soon, turn sharply RIGHT onto a stony track which goes uphill through trees. Ignore a track going right as the main track levels off and turns LEFT. The track then climbs again (ignore a minor left-turn) and turns sharply RIGHT (ignore the path going ahead here). Soon turn LEFT at a junction with a surfaced track leading to a house.

Known as Tŷ Mawr, this was the Gwynfynydd mine manager's house. It was built near the gold workings which were begun in 1887.

5 The track goes uphill and immediately turns sharp RIGHT (ignore the grass track going left). Continue uphill above Tŷ Mawr, passing wooden fencing surrounding a mine adit and going through a gateway. Soon turn RIGHT onto a tarmac road and walk the short distance back to your car.

WALK 13

RHAEADR MAWDDACH & PONT GWYNFYNDD

DESCRIPTION This dramatic 2½-mile walk passes through the upper workings of the famous Gwynfynydd gold mine before descending to the Afon Mawddach. It then takes you to impressive waterfalls both on that river and on the nearby Afon Gain, before climbing to a remote bridge over the Gain on the way to Gwynfynydd Farm. Allow 3 hours.

START Parking space above the Afon Mawddach near Bedd y Coedwr Farm. SH 736285.

DIRECTIONS *From Dolgellau:* Take the A470 towards Porthmadog and Blaenau Ffestiniog. Enter Coed y Brenin soon after Llanelltyd and pass the Ty'n y Groes Hotel on the left before going through Ganllwyd. Soon after the village pass the entrance to the Coed y Brenin Visitor Centre on the right and, after another two miles, turn RIGHT on to a minor road at Bronaber. Follow this road (signposted Llanuwchllyn/Abergeirw) through Trawsfynydd Holiday Village, ignoring a right turn for the Rhiwgoch pub. Bear RIGHT just past Penystryd Farm, cross a cattle-grid and then immediately turn RIGHT onto a road where there's a dead-end sign. Pass Penystryd chapel and go downhill to bridge the Afon Gain before entering Coed y Brenin. Continue uphill through the forest, passing a right turn signposted for cycle track 8 and then, also on the right, the track going to Gwynfynnyd Farm. Pass open fields, and then a track descending on the right. Park soon after this in a clearing in the trees on the LEFT. *From Porthmadog:* Take the A487 (subsequently the A470) towards Dolgellau. Pass Trawsfynydd and, after two miles, turn LEFT onto a minor road at Bronaber. Follow this road (signposted Llanuwchllyn/Abergeirw) through Trawsfynydd Holiday Village, ignoring a right turn for the Rhiwgoch pub. Bear RIGHT just past Penystryd Farm, cross a cattle-grid and then immediately turn RIGHT onto a road where there's a dead-end sign. Pass Penystryd chapel and go downhill to bridge the Afon Gain before entering Coed y Brenin. Continue uphill through the forest, passing a right turn signposted for cycle track 8 and then, also on the right, the track going to Gwynfynnyd Farm. Pass open fields, and then a track descending on the right. Park soon after this in a clearing in the trees on the LEFT.

1 Go RIGHT and follow the road uphill to a track on the left. Turn LEFT here, go downhill through trees, through a gateway and between wooden fencing to pass above a house on the left. *This is Tŷ Mawr, where the manager of Gwynfynydd gold mine once lived. The mine was named after the farm of Gwynfynydd which you will pass later.* When the track bends left continue AHEAD on a fenced, grassy track, passing through a wooden gateway and across a path at right angles near a mine-shaft. The track then descends to a wooden gateway.

2 Go through the gateway, following a path, alongside a wall, downhill through cleared forest. The path bends right and reaches a footpath sign and yellow marker, on the right. Go LEFT here, crossing a cycle track and passing another yellow marker. Soon you reach a forestry track alongside a bridge over the Afon Mawddach.

3 Turn RIGHT onto the track and walk downhill. *Soon you will see the spectacular Mawddach waterfalls, followed by buildings belonging to the Gwynfynydd gold mine, on the left. Gold was first discovered at Gwynfynydd in 1863. However, finds were subsequently sporadic until, in 1887, a lode containing good quality gold was found on the hillside above the falls, near the mine manager's house.* Pass a red footpath marker and ignore a left turn as the track bears right to arrive at a bridge. *Look to the right as you cross to see the dramatic Pistyll Cain waterfalls.*

4 After the bridge, pass a yellow marker then go RIGHT by a red marker onto a

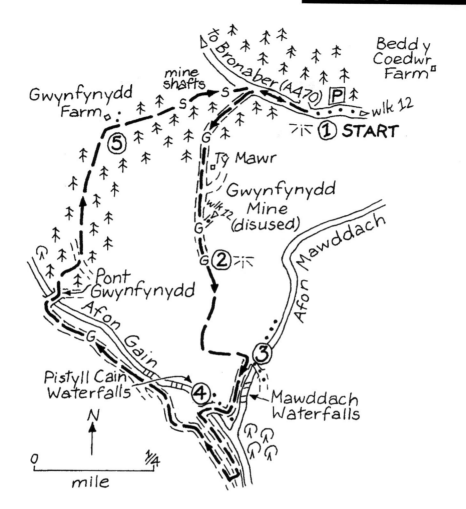

path going uphill to meet a grassy track. Here turn RIGHT by another red marker, passing a path going left as you walk uphill. After a wooden gate turn RIGHT onto a forestry track which goes downhill to Pont Gwynfynydd over the Afon Gain. At the far end of the bridge ignore a footpath sign indicating right and go LEFT onto a path leading uphill through the trees. At a forestry track go LEFT for a short distance, ignoring a footpath sign indicating right. Then go RIGHT and follow a track uphill. This passes a wall on the right before reaching Gwynfynydd Farm.

5 Ignore a grass track going right shortly before the main track bends left to the farm gate. Instead, walk AHEAD uphill to the right of the farm gate and fence. Go between the trees, to the left of an old wooden seat, on a path which gradually bears away from the fence. Pass a fenced-off mine shaft on the left, then go LEFT and cross a stile. Turn RIGHT and walk alongside the fence past another mine shaft. Go RIGHT over another stile and LEFT to reach a tarmac road. Turn RIGHT and walk back to your car.

TYDDYN MAWR & AFON MAWDDACH

DESCRIPTION This delightful 4-mile walk takes you from the tiny hamlet of Abergeirw to a point high above the Mawddach river from where there are good views of Coed y Brenin and the Rhinog mountains. On the return you pass the ancient farmhouse of Pant Glas and look across to the summit of Rhobell Fawr as you descend to the Mawddach valley. Allow 3½ hours.

START Parking space near the bridge over the Afon Mawddach at Abergeirw. SH 768291.

DIRECTIONS *From Dolgellau:* Take the A470 northwards towards Porthmadog and Blaenau Ffestiniog. Enter Coed y Brenin soon after Llanelltyd and pass the Ty'n y Groes Hotel on the left before going through Ganllwyd. Soon after the village pass the entrance to the Coed y Brenin Visitor Centre on the right and, after another two miles, turn RIGHT on to a minor road at Bronaber. Follow this road (signposted Llanuwchllyn/Abergeirw) through Trawsfynydd Holiday Village, ignoring a right turn for the Rhiwgoch pub. Bear RIGHT just past Penystryd Farm, cross a cattle-grid and continue AHEAD on the main road. Go downhill, RIGHT at a junction (signposted Abergeirw/ Dolgellau/Llanfachreth) and cross the Afon Gain. The road then climbs steeply before, after two miles, descending to the bridge over the Afon Mawddach at Abergeirw. Park on the RIGHT after the bridge. *From Porthmadog:* Take the A487 (subsequently the A470) towards Dolgellau. Pass Trawsfynydd and, after two miles, turn LEFT onto a minor road at Bronaber. Follow this road (signposted Llanuwchllyn/Abergeirw) through Trawsfynydd Holiday Village, ignoring a right turn for the Rhiwgoch pub. Bear right just past Penystryd Farm, cross a cattle-grid and continue AHEAD on the main road. Go downhill, RIGHT at a junction (signposted Abergeirw/ Dolgellau/Llanfachreth) and cross the Afon Gain. The road then climbs steeply before, after two

miles, descending to the bridge over the Afon Mawddach at Abergeirw. Park on the RIGHT after the bridge.

1 Cross the bridge and go RIGHT at a footpath sign. Follow the track over another bridge, past Abergeirw chapel and through a wooden gate. Walk uphill to a house, bear to the RIGHT of it and make for a gate with a yellow marker, just beyond it. Turn LEFT here and follow the fence alongside the house, passing another marker before bearing RIGHT to go uphill through the forest. Soon bear LEFT at a marker (watch out for this) and continue uphill to a forestry track.

2 Turn LEFT here (ignore the marker opposite: the right-of-way it indicates becomes difficult to find) and follow the road to a clearing with a communications mast. *Pause here for a good view of the domed summit of Rhobell Fawr and the pointed lower summit of Rhobell y Big.* Continue uphill to a junction and a yellow marker. Turn RIGHT here to continue uphill, soon passing some ruined buildings below to the right. *Before long there are spectacular views of the upper Mawddach valley to the east. High above the Mawddach to the north-west you will also see the settlements of Bryn y Gath and Pant Glas, which you will pass later.* Before long the forestry road ends.

3 Continue AHEAD on a path past a marker and follow it downhill. Soon cross a wooden footbridge and go through a gap in a wall to arrive at a forestry track. Turn RIGHT onto the track, as indicated by a marker with a blue arrow on a yellow background, and follow the track as it bends left and goes uphill. *After the brow of the hill there's a wonderful view over Coed y Brenin to the Rhinog mountains ahead. The three main peaks are Y Lethr (to the left), Rhinog Fach (ahead) and Rhinog Fawr (to the right).* Ignore a right turn as you descend from the hilltop and continue AHEAD on the track, passing another blue marker. At the point where the track bears left and goes uphill again take a path going HALF-RIGHT as indicated by the blue marker. Follow the path downhill to arrive at a wooden gate

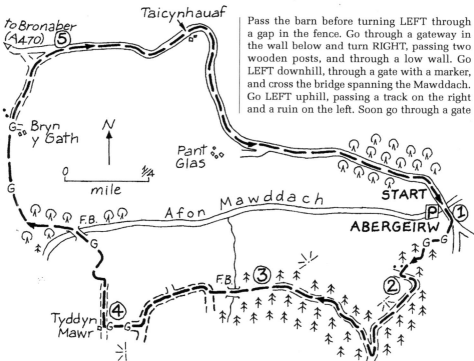

Pass the barn before turning LEFT through a gap in the fence. Go through a gateway in the wall below and turn RIGHT, passing two wooden posts, and through a low wall. Go LEFT downhill, through a gate with a marker, and cross the bridge spanning the Mawddach. Go LEFT uphill, passing a track on the right and a ruin on the left. Soon go through a gate

by a blue marker. Go through and continue AHEAD, walking downhill alongside a fence before bearing RIGHT to another blue marker. As you approach the marker Tyddyn Mawr comes into sight below you. Descend from this point to a gateway and marker alongside the house.

4 Go through the gateway, turn RIGHT onto the track behind the house and make for a barn. Soon go through another gateway with marker and walk downhill.

by another ruin, then walk uphill to another gate near Bryn y Gath house. Once through, walk between the barn and house, then turn LEFT onto a track going uphill. Go RIGHT at a junction to a tarmac road.

5 Turn RIGHT and follow the road past the ruins of Taicynhauaf and then Pant Glas Farm (both on the right). *Please note the right-of-way between Bryn y Gath and Pant Glas is out of use.* The road then descends steeply to Abergeirw.

AROUND HERMON

DESCRIPTION A 2½-mile walk on which you explore the idyllic countryside which surrounds the remote village of Hermon. A delightful woodland path takes you high above the village, after which you descend to the farm of Cae'n y Coed, deep in the forest park. After this, you visit the site of the extraordinary Hermon turf copper mine before climbing to a viewpoint over the Mawddach valley on the way back to the village. Allow 2½ hours.

START Forestry Commission Wales car park (free) at Hermon. SH 749256.

DIRECTIONS *From Dolgellau:* Take the A470 northwards towards Porthmadog and Blaenau Ffestiniog. Enter Coed y Brenin soon after Llanelltyd and shortly after passing the Ty'n y Groes Hotel on the left turn RIGHT onto a minor road signposted Llanfachreth/Abergeirw. Cross the Afon Mawddach and follow the road RIGHT at the Ty'n y Groes picnic site. Go LEFT at the first junction (no signpost) and follow the road uphill. Pass through two gates (usually open) and ignore several tracks to left and right before reaching a junction by the Dolfrwynog Tea Gardens. Turn RIGHT and drive downhill to the Hermon forestry car park on the LEFT. *From Porthmadog:* Take the A487 (subsequently the A470) towards Dolgellau. Pass Trawsfynydd and Bronaber before entering Coed y Brenin. You'll see the entrance to the forest park visitor centre on the left before reaching Ganllwyd. Drive through the village and turn LEFT onto a minor road (signposted Llanfachreth/Abergeirw) about ¼-mile beyond it. Cross the Afon Mawddach and follow the road RIGHT at the Ty'n y Groes picnic site. Go LEFT at the first junction (no signpost) and follow the road uphill. Pass through two gates (usually open) and ignore several tracks to left and right before reaching a junction by the Dolfrwynog Tea Gardens. Turn RIGHT and drive downhill to the Hermon forestry car park on the LEFT.

1 Turn RIGHT onto the road and find, on the right of the second entrance to the forestry track on the left, a footpath sign. Join a path here which goes uphill a short distance to another path. Go LEFT onto this path and follow it uphill, ignoring a cycle track below it. *Pause as you climb for a good view over the valley of the Afon Wen to Pen y Bryn house* (see **Walk 18**), *high on the hillside above it.* Soon the path levels off and goes alongside a fence before joining the cycle track and passing through a low wall. Take care here because the path goes HALF-LEFT off the cycle track immediately after the wall. Check for the marker post a short distance along the path.

2 The path climbs, then passes some fencing before reaching a junction with a path on the left. Continue AHEAD, cross a cycle track then arrive at a forestry track where there are markers. Turn RIGHT and follow the track uphill. Pass an orange marker, after which the track descends to a gate and tarmac road.

3 Go LEFT onto the road and then RIGHT onto a bridleway. This goes uphill (ignore left and right turns) to near Cae'n y Coed house. Follow path diversion signs now. Go LEFT above the house then RIGHT down to the boundary fence. Walk LEFT through a wall and down to a track. Turn RIGHT onto this, ignore paths on the left and a track on the right, and arrive at a gate.

4 Turn LEFT and follow the track downhill, ignoring a track on the left and marked path going right. Soon you reach the site (on the right) of the Hermon turf copper mine. *The peat on the hillside above you is so rich in copper that, during the early 19th century, it was cut from the hill and burnt here in a stone kiln. The ash was then transported all the way to Swansea for smelting.* Continue on the track to a junction. Here, turn sharp RIGHT and walk uphill through initially cleared forest. Ignore a marked path, then a grass track, on the right, before reaching a junction. Turn RIGHT here onto an uphill track which takes you to Bwlchrhoswen Isaf house on the left. *Pause here for splendid*

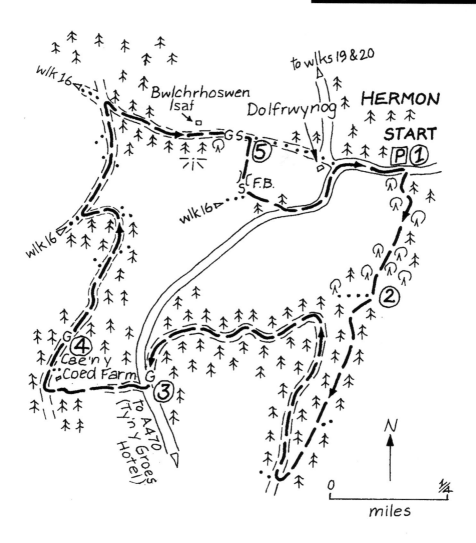

views to the left over Coed y Brenin and the Mawddach valley.

5 Soon after Bwlchrhoswen Isaf there's a gate and stile on the right. Turn RIGHT here and walk down the field beyond, going HALF-LEFT towards some trees and a stream. Turn LEFT just before the trees, cross the stream, then go RIGHT down to cross a stile and wooden bridge. Follow a grassy path LEFT through a wall towards a yellow marker. Here, turn LEFT, and go through another wall. Then walk uphill to a tarmac road where there's a white marker and a footpath sign. Go LEFT onto the road, through a gate, and then follow it to a junction by the Dolfrwynog Tea Gardens *(call 01341 440239 for opening times)*. Turn RIGHT to return to the car park at Hermon.

BWLCHRHOSWEN ISAF & AFON MAWDDACH

DESCRIPTION A 3½-mile walk which takes you from Hermon, a tiny village at the heart of Coed y Brenin, down to spectacular rapids and gorges on the Afon Mawddach. You cross the Mawddach twice, on footbridges high above the river, and return to Hermon on a route which passes the site of an extraordinary turf copper mine. Allow 3½ hours.

START Forestry Commission Wales car park (free) at Hermon. SH 749256.

DIRECTIONS *From Dolgellau:* Take the A470 northwards towards Porthmadog and Blaenau Ffestiniog. Enter Coed y Brenin soon after Llanelltyd and shortly after passing the Ty'n y Groes Hotel on the left turn RIGHT onto a minor road signposted Llanfachreth/Abergeirw. Cross the Afon Mawddach and follow the road RIGHT at the Ty'n y Groes picnic site. Go LEFT at the first junction (no signpost) and follow the road uphill. Pass through two gates (usually open) and ignore several tracks to left and right before reaching a junction by the Dolfrwynog Tea Gardens. Turn RIGHT and drive downhill to the Hermon forestry car park on the LEFT. *From Porthmadog:* Take the A487 (subsequently the A470) towards Dolgellau. Pass Trawsfynydd and Bronaber before entering Coed y Brenin. You'll see the entrance to the forest park visitor centre on the left before reaching Ganllwyd. Drive through the village and turn LEFT onto a minor road (signposted Llanfachreth/Abergeirw) about ¼-mile beyond it. Cross the Afon Mawddach and follow the road RIGHT at the Ty'n y Groes picnic site. Go LEFT at the first junction (no signpost) and follow the road uphill. Pass through two gates (usually open) and ignore several tracks to left and right before reaching a junction by the Dolfrwynog Tea Gardens. Turn RIGHT and drive downhill to the Hermon forestry car park on the LEFT.

1 Turn RIGHT from the car park onto the tarmac road. Walk uphill past tracks going left and a road on the left just before the Dolfrwynog Tea Gardens *(call 01341 440239 for opening times)*. Take the track going LEFT after the café and follow it, ignoring a path at right angles, to the old settlement of Bwlchrhoswen Isaf on the right. *This section of track offers splendid views to the left over Coed y Brenin to Y Garn. This peak, which belongs to the Rhinog mountain range, towers above the village of Ganllwyd* (see **Walks 1-6**).

2 Continue downhill into the forest, going AHEAD at a junction of tracks and through a gate. Pass a blue marker on the left and reach a forestry information panel on the right. *This draws attention to the ancient middle Cambrian silt stones in the cliffs above you.* Continue on the track, watching for a cycle track on the left immediately before you turn sharp LEFT onto a path by a yellow marker. This goes through the trees down to a forestry track by yellow markers.

3 Turn RIGHT here and follow the track above the Afon Mawddach to a wooden foot-bridge on the left. Go LEFT downhill near a wooden seat and across the bridge. *Pause here for a dramatic view of the Mawddach river far below you. During the floods in 2001 the river rose more than 10m and washed away the old stone bridge upstream at Abergeirw (see* **Walk 14**). Go LEFT uphill at the end of the bridge and then LEFT onto a tarmac road. Follow this alongside the river for a few minutes to a car park on the left. Turn LEFT here, pass some forestry information boards, and cross Pont Cae'n y Coed, another footbridge suspended high above the Mawddach

4 At the end of the bridge go LEFT by a white and yellow marker onto a forestry track. Follow this uphill to a junction. Go RIGHT here past a white and green marker and continue uphill. Ignore a cycle track on the left and a blue marker on the right before reaching another junction in cleared forest. Keep RIGHT here past an orange marker and follow the track as it goes to the right uphill.

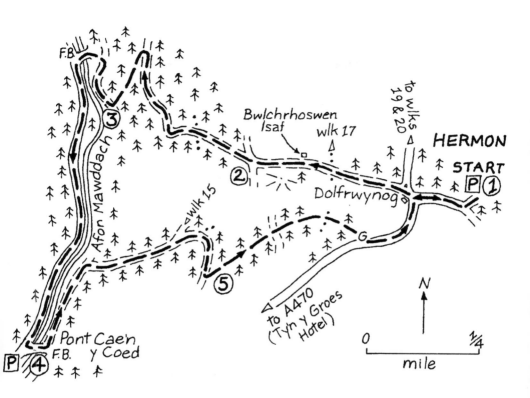

Soon you'll reach the site of the Hermon turf copper mine on the left. *The peat on the hillside above you is so rich in copper that, during the early 19th century, it was cut from the hill and burnt here in a stone kiln. The ash was then transported all the way to Swansea for smelting.* Continue on the track until you reach a path going LEFT at an orange marker.

5 Follow this path past a blue marker uphill alongside a wall on the right. Ignore a path going left and then one going right at an orange marker. Then ignore another path going left at a yellow marker and walk uphill until you reach a tarmac road where there's a white marker and a footpath sign. Go LEFT onto the road, through a gate, and then follow it to a junction by the Dolfrwynog Tea Gardens. Turn RIGHT to return to the car park at Hermon.

WALK 17

CWMHEISIAN ISAF & PISTYLL CAIN

DESCRIPTION On this 4-mile walk you climb up into the hills above the secluded village of Hermon and are rewarded with wonderful views over the village to the mountains of Rhobell Fawr and Cadair Idris. Soon after, you reach another viewpoint, above Cwmheisian Isaf farmhouse, from where the majestic Pistyll Cain waterfalls can be seen (and heard) a mile away. The walk then takes you to both the Mawddach and Gain falls before returning to Hermon. Allow 3½ hours.

START Forestry Commission Wales car park (free) at Hermon. SH 749256.

DIRECTIONS *From Dolgellau:* Take the A470 northwards towards Porthmadog and Blaenau Ffestiniog. Enter Coed y Brenin soon after Llanelltyd and shortly after passing the Ty'n y Groes Hotel on the left turn RIGHT onto a minor road signposted Llanfachreth/Abergeirw. Cross the Afon Mawddach and follow the road RIGHT at the Ty'n y Groes picnic site. Go LEFT at the first junction (no signpost) and follow the road uphill. Pass through two gates (usually open) and ignore several tracks to left and right before reaching a junction by the Dolfrwynog Tea Gardens. Turn RIGHT and drive downhill to the Hermon forestry car park on the LEFT. *From Porthmadog:* Take the A487 (subsequently the A470) towards Dolgellau. Pass Trawsfynydd and Bronaber before entering Coed y Brenin. You'll see the entrance to the forest park visitor centre on the left before reaching Ganllwyd. Drive through the village and turn LEFT onto a minor road signposted Llanfachreth/Abergeirw about ¼-mile beyond it. Cross the Afon Mawddach and follow the road RIGHT at the Ty'n y Groes picnic site. Go LEFT at the first junction (no signpost) and follow the road uphill. Pass through two gates (usually open) and ignore several tracks to left and right before reaching a junction by the Dolfrwynog Tea Gardens. Turn RIGHT and drive downhill to the Hermon forestry car park on the LEFT.

1 Turn RIGHT from the car park onto the tarmac road. Walk uphill past tracks going left and a road on the left just before the Dolfrwynog Tea Gardens *(call 01341 440239 for opening times)*. Take the track going LEFT after the café and follow it to a metal gate, and stile, on the right at the top of a short rise. Go RIGHT at the gate and uphill, soon bearing HALF-LEFT to a stile. Cross this, go through a wall and then to the RIGHT of ruined buildings. Walk AHEAD uphill to a stile. Cross this and continue alongside a wall on the right. Soon pass a yellow marker on the left and reach Ty'n y Simdde house.

2 Go LEFT in front of the house, then RIGHT onto a grass track which takes you past Ty'n y Simdde to a tarmac road. Go LEFT uphill to a junction with forestry tracks. Turn LEFT, passing a green and white marker. *Pause here for a magnificent view of the summit of Rhobell Fawr to the left and the ridge of Cadair Idris to the right.* Follow the track past two yellow markers into the forest. Pass a sign saying 'Araf/Slow', a cycle track crossing and a grass track on the right before reaching a clearing above Cwmheisian Isaf to the left. *From here you can see the spectacular Pistyll Cain waterfalls to the north.*

3 Continue downhill, ignoring a marked path going right. At a sharp left bend go RIGHT onto a track which passes a cycle track on the left and descends to a ford. Cross the stream on a stone slab to the right and follow the track downhill to a junction above the Afon Mawddach. Go LEFT then immediately RIGHT downhill by a white and yellow marker to a bridge over the Mawddach.

4 Go LEFT at the bridge end and downhill. *Soon you will see the spectacular Mawddach waterfalls, then buildings belonging to the Gwynfynydd gold mine, on the left.* Pass a red marker and a left turn before arriving at a bridge over the Afon Gain. Go RIGHT here to view the Pistyll Cain waterfalls. Cross the bridge, pass a yellow marker and a path going right, and continue to the settlement of Ferndale *(for self-catering holiday accommodation here tel: 01341 440247 or email: pennywood@coedybrenin.com)*.

5 Pass a barrier and houses on the right, go through a metal gate and soon join a tarmac road. Continue on the road, passing Tyddyn Gwladys car park and tracks to left then right. Soon, go LEFT downhill, then RIGHT onto a gravel path below the road. Follow this to a wooden bridge across the Mawddach.

6 Continue AHEAD after crossing, then go RIGHT onto a track by an orange marker. Soon, at yellow markers, go LEFT uphill through the forest to another track. Turn RIGHT here by a yellow marker and pass a cycle track before reaching a forestry information panel. *This draws attention to the ancient middle Cambrian silt stones in the cliffs above you.* Continue, passing a blue marker and a gate before going AHEAD at a junction to reach Bwlchrhoswen Isaf. Then follow the track back to Hermon.

Map labels:
Pistyll Gain ④
Afon Gain
Mawddach waterfalls
ford
wlks 19820
Cwmheisian Isaf ③
Ferndale ⑤
Afon Mawddach
FB
⑥
Ty'n y Simdde
②
s
to wlks 19820
HERMON
START
P ①
Bwlchrhoswen Isaf
G/S
Dolfrwynog
to A470
N
0   ¼
mile

33

AFON WEN & PEN Y BRYN

DESCRIPTION A fine 3-mile walk which takes you to an idyllic spot by a footbridge over the Afon Wen before climbing alongside a tributary of the Wen to one of the most spectacular viewpoints in Coed y Brenin. On the way you skirt a deep ravine, and cross a stream near a series of dramatic waterfalls in the forest high above the Wen valley. Allow 3½ hours.

START Forestry Commission Wales car park (free) in Hermon. SH 749256.

DIRECTIONS *From Dolgellau:* Take the A470 northwards towards Porthmadog and Blaenau Ffestiniog. Enter Coed y Brenin soon after Llanelltyd and shortly after passing the Ty'n y Groes Hotel on the left turn RIGHT onto a minor road signposted Llanfachreth/Abergeirw. Cross the Afon Mawddach and follow the road RIGHT at the Ty'n y Groes picnic site. Go LEFT at the first junction (no signpost) and follow the road uphill. Pass through two gates (usually open) and ignore several tracks to left and right before reaching a junction by the Dolfrwynog Tea Gardens. Turn RIGHT and drive downhill to the Hermon forestry car park on the LEFT. *From Porthmadog:* Take the A487 (subsequently the A470) towards Dolgellau. Pass Trawsfynydd and Bronaber before entering Coed y Brenin. You'll see the entrance to the forest park visitor centre on the left before reaching Ganllwyd. Drive through the village and turn LEFT onto a minor road (signposted Llanfachreth/Abergeirw) about ¼-mile beyond it. Cross the Afon Mawddach and follow the road RIGHT at the Ty'n y Groes picnic site. Go LEFT at the first junction (no signpost) and follow the road uphill. Pass through two gates (usually open) and ignore several tracks to left and right before reaching a junction by the Dolfrwynog Tea Gardens. Turn RIGHT and drive downhill to the Hermon forestry car park on the LEFT.

I Cross the road and take the forestry track opposite, going through a metal gate. Soon there's another gateway followed by a forestry information board. *This informs us that Hermon lies at the centre of what was once the Rhobell volcano and that the locality is famous for one of the oldest porphyry-copper deposits in the world. Indeed the area immediately to the right of the track at this point has been made a Site of Special Scientific Interest for this very reason.* Continue on the track, passing a path going right before arriving at a yellow marker on the left. Go LEFT here and follow a path downhill to cross a bridge over the Afon Wen. *The Wen, with the Mawddach and Eden, is one of the three main rivers of Coed y Brenin. The waterfall and deep pool to the left of the bridge make this an idyllic spot.* Continue uphill to reach a tarmac road alongside a footpath sign.

2 Cross the road and follow a marked path going HALF-RIGHT uphill through cleared forest. Ignore a faint path going left and continue into the forest. The path climbs more steeply before bearing left and crossing a bridge over a tributary of the Wen. *There are some magnificent waterfalls on this tributary which you will cross again later. The precipitous gorge which contains the falls is known as Ceunant Hyll (Awesome Ravine).* Follow the path as it zig-zags uphill. Soon it levels off and passes a yellow marker before reaching a junction with a track where there are white and yellow markers.

3 Turn LEFT here, as indicated by the yellow marker, and follow a grassy track to its end in a turning circle. Cross this and continue AHEAD on an uphill path which goes through a wall above a waterfall on the tributary stream of the Wen. The path then descends left to cross the stream by the remains of a bridge (take care), after which it continues left directly above the waterfalls. Soon the path emerges from the trees and crosses a grass and heather-covered hilltop. *This hilltop provides one of the finest viewpoints in Coed y Brenin. The entire Rhinog mountain ridge can be seen to the west, with the lower Mawddach valley and Cadair Idris to the south-west.*

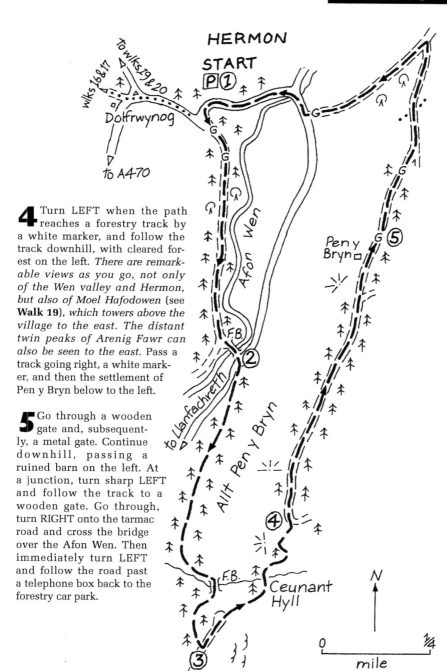

4 Turn LEFT when the path reaches a forestry track by a white marker, and follow the track downhill, with cleared forest on the left. *There are remarkable views as you go, not only of the Wen valley and Hermon, but also of Moel Hafodowen (see* **Walk 19**), *which towers above the village to the east. The distant twin peaks of Arenig Fawr can also be seen to the east.* Pass a track going right, a white marker, and then the settlement of Pen y Bryn below to the left.

5 Go through a wooden gate and, subsequently, a metal gate. Continue downhill, passing a ruined barn on the left. At a junction, turn sharp LEFT and follow the track to a wooden gate. Go through, turn RIGHT onto the tarmac road and cross the bridge over the Afon Wen. Then immediately turn LEFT and follow the road past a telephone box back to the forestry car park.

35

WALK 19

CWMHEISIAN ISAF & MOEL HAFODOWEN

DESCRIPTION This varied 5-mile walk takes you past the farmhouse of Cwmheisian Isaf, high above the confluence of the Afon Mawddach with the Afon Gain, to the hills above the village of Hermon in the Wen valley. The climax of the walk is your arrival at a viewpoint near the summit of Moel Hafodowen which provides wide-ranging views over the forest. Allow 4 hours.

START Junction of three tracks with the tarmac road above Cwmheisian Ganol. SH 744273. There's space for two cars on the right of the second track going left.

DIRECTIONS *From Dolgellau:* Take the A470 northwards towards Porthmadog and Blaenau Ffestiniog. Enter Coed y Brenin soon after Llanelltyd and shortly after passing the Ty'n y Groes Hotel on the left turn RIGHT onto a minor road signposted Llanfachreth/Abergeirw. Cross the Afon Mawddach and follow the road RIGHT at the Ty'n y Groes picnic site. Go LEFT at the first junction (no signpost) and follow the road uphill. Pass through two gates (usually open) and ignore several tracks to left and right before reaching a junction by the Dolfrwynog Tea Gardens. Turn LEFT and drive past the café and uphill on the tarmac road, passing several tracks to left and right. When the road levels off drive for another mile or so until the road bears left above cleared forestry also on the left. Park at a junction with tracks where the road turns right to go uphill. *From Porthmadog:* Take the A487 (subsequently the A470) towards Dolgellau. Pass Trawsfynydd and Bronaber before entering Coed y Brenin. You'll see the entrance to the forest park visitor centre on the left before reaching Ganllwyd. Drive through the village and turn LEFT onto a minor road (signposted Llanfachreth/Abergeirw) about ¼-mile beyond it. Cross the Afon Mawddach and follow the road RIGHT at the Ty'n y Groes picnic site. Go LEFT at the first junction (no signpost) and follow the road uphill. Pass through two gates (usually open) and ignore several tracks to left and right before reaching a junction by the Dolfrwynog Tea Gardens. Turn LEFT and drive past the café and uphill on the tarmac road, passing several tracks to left and right. When the road levels off drive for another mile or so until the road bears left above cleared forestry also on the left. Park at a junction with tracks where the road turns right to go uphill.

1 Walk back along the tarmac road for a short distance and turn RIGHT onto a path going downhill alongside cleared forest on the right. Pass three yellow markers then signs pointing left to the 'Ffordd Cyngor/ Council Road' before reaching a forest track. Turn LEFT and follow the track uphill above the settlement of Cwmheisian Isaf on the right. *From here you can see (and hear) the spectacular Pistyll Cain waterfalls (see* **Walks 10, 13** *and* **17**) *a mile away to the north. These falls take the Afon Gain down to join the Afon Mawddach in a dramatic setting in the midst of Coed y Brenin.*

2 Enter the forest, passing a grass track on the right and a cycle track crossing. After the track reaches a clearing on the right pass two yellow markers to arrive at a tarmac road by a green and white marker. *Pause here for a magnificent view of the summit of Rhobell Fawr.*

3 Cross the road and continue HALF-RIGHT on the track opposite. This takes you downhill to a junction in the forest where you should turn LEFT and pass above the settlement of Buarthre. Ignore a path going left just after the house and continue uphill on the track which soon enters a section where the forest has been cleared on the right. Continue as the track levels off and begins to descend. *There are good views from here of the twin peaks of Arenig Fawr (ahead on the right) and of its neighbour Moel Lyfnant (on the left).* Go LEFT onto a tarmac road and follow this a short distance before turning LEFT again onto a path/cycle track going uphill through trees.

4 At a junction turn LEFT, as indicated by the cycle track markers. Follow the

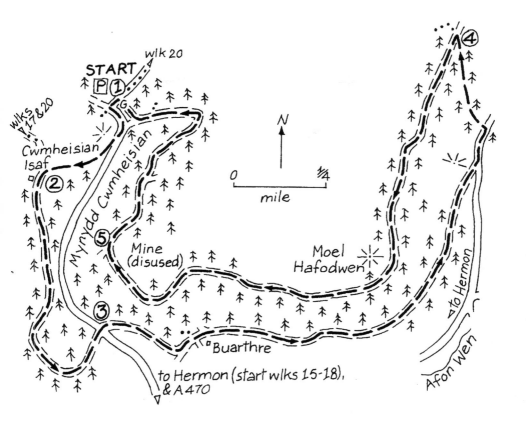

track uphill until, after emerging from the forest, it reaches a viewpoint near the summit of Moel Hafodowen before beginning to descend. *Moel Hafodowen is the highest point in Coed y Brenin and, from here, there are spectacular views over Coed y Brenin to the surrounding mountains. These include Rhobell Fawr (to the south), Cadair Idris (to the south-west) and the Rhinog ridge (to the west).* Soon, ignore a path going left and pass a forestry information board. The track continues downhill, eventually arriving at a junction of tracks below mine workings on the right.

5 Turn RIGHT here and walk uphill, following a track which levels off at a passing place. Ignore a track going right and continue AHEAD, following the main track as it winds its way downhill. Go through a gateway to a tarmac road. Cross this to reach your car.

HAFOD FRAITH & RHAEADR MAWDDACH

DESCRIPTION A 4-mile walk which takes you from the hills above the Afon Mawddach down to the spectacular waterfalls at the confluence of the Mawddach and Afon Gain. An old bridleway then takes you back up into the hills where, near the old settlement of Cwmheisian Ganol, you gain wonderful views of the Rhinog mountains. Allow 3½ hours.

START Junction of three tracks with the tarmac road above Cwmheisian Ganol. SH 744273. There's space for two cars on the right of the second track going left.

DIRECTIONS *From Dolgellau:* Take the A470 northwards towards Porthmadog and Blaenau Ffestiniog. Enter Coed y Brenin soon after Llanelltyd and shortly after passing the Ty'n y Groes Hotel on the left turn RIGHT onto a minor road signposted Llanfachreth/Abergeirw. Cross the Afon Mawddach and follow the road RIGHT at the Ty'n y Groes picnic site. Go LEFT at the first junction (no signpost) and follow the road uphill. Pass through two gates (usually open) and ignore several tracks to left and right before reaching a junction by the Dolfrwynog Tea Gardens. Turn LEFT and drive past the café and uphill on the tarmac road, passing several tracks to left and right. When the road levels off drive for another mile or so until the road bears left above cleared forestry also on the left. Park at a junction with tracks where the road turns right to go uphill. *From Porthmadog:* Take the A487 (subsequently the A470) towards Dolgellau. Pass Trawsfynydd and Bronaber before entering Coed y Brenin. You'll see the entrance to the forest park visitor centre on the left before reaching Ganllwyd. Drive through the village and turn LEFT onto a minor road (signposted Llanfachreth/Abergeirw) about ¼-mile beyond it. Cross the Afon Mawddach and a cattle grid, and follow the road RIGHT at the Ty'n y Groes picnic site. Go LEFT at the first junction (no signpost) and follow the

road uphill. Pass through two gates (usually open) and ignore several tracks to left and right before reaching a junction by the Dolfrwynog Tea Gardens. Turn LEFT and drive past the café and uphill on the tarmac road, passing several tracks to left and right. When the road levels off drive for another mile or so until the road bears left above cleared forestry also on the left. Park at a junction with tracks where the road turns right to go uphill.

1 Walk uphill on the tarmac road and enter the Hafod Fraith estate (this a right of way so don't be worried by the 'private' notice). Continue on the road, going through a wooden gateway before passing Hafod Fraith house and, after a cattle grid, Hendre Perfedd. *Stop here for a glorious view, to the west, of the three central peaks of the Rhinog mountain range.* Continue on a grass track, going through a gateway before reaching Tyddyn Mawr house.

2 Go through the gateway before the house, then turn sharp LEFT at a marker post. Walk downhill and go through a gateway to another marker. Continue downhill to markers by a stream. Go RIGHT over the stream then LEFT downhill alongside it. Bear RIGHT at another marker before reaching a metal gate. Go through, over the stream and immediately through another gateway with marker. Go AHEAD alongside the forest fence, through a wooden gate by a marker and follow a track to a metal gate. Walk through into the forest, crossing two streams. The track then descends to the Mawddach, passing waterfalls on the left.

3 At a junction bear RIGHT, then go through a wooden gate and RIGHT onto a forest track. *Watch out for wooden fencing to the right over the river. This encloses part* *of the Bedd y Coedwr gold mine, originally named after a nearby farmhouse (see* **Walk 12**). *Soon, pass a ford across the Mawddach and follow the track to a junction. On the left is a bridleway to which you will return later.*

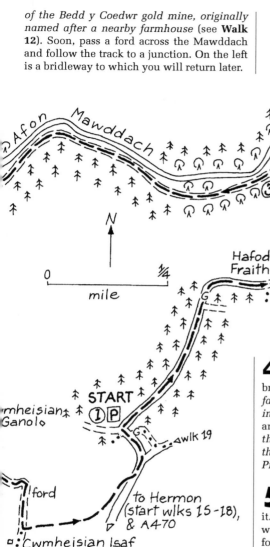

4 For now, go RIGHT and cross the Afon Mawddach. Go LEFT after the stone bridge. *Soon you'll see the Mawddach waterfalls, then the Gwynfynydd gold mine buildings, on the left.* Pass a red footpath marker and go RIGHT to another bridge. *This spans the Afon Gain. Walk a few yards uphill to the right of the bridge for a good view of the Pistyll Cain waterfalls.*

5 Return the way you came, going RIGHT over the Mawddach to the junction above it. Turn LEFT, then RIGHT onto the bridleway, which climbs before entering cleared forest. *Here Y Garn, one of the Rhinog range, dominates the view to the right. Above you, on the left, is the settlement of Cwmheisian Ganol.* Soon, cross a ford on a stone slab bridge, then pass a cycle trail and reach a forest track. Turn LEFT and go uphill to a sign marked 'Ffordd Cyngor'. Turn LEFT here and go AHEAD, passing a yellow marker and another 'Council Road' sign. Walk uphill past two yellow markers to a tarmac road. Turn LEFT to reach your car.

PRONUNCIATION

Welsh	English equivalent
c	always hard, as in **cat**
ch	as in the Scottish word lo**ch**
dd	as th in **then**
f	as f in o**f**
ff	as ff in o**ff**
g	always hard as in **got**
ll	no real equivalent. It is like 'th' in then, but with an 'L' sound added to it, giving 'thlan' for the pronunciation of the Welsh 'Llan'.

In Welsh the accent usually falls on the last-but-one syllable of a word.

KEY TO THE MAPS

- **→** Walk route and direction
- ▬ Metalled road
- --- Unsurfaced road
- •••• Footpath/route adjoining walk route
- ⌇ River/stream
- ⚘ ♤ Trees
- ▬ Railway
- **G** Gate
- **S** Stile
- **F.B.** Footbridge
- ☀ Viewpoint
- **P** Parking

THE COUNTRYSIDE CODE

- Be safe – plan ahead and follow any signs
- Leave gates and property as you find them
- Protect plants and animals, and take your litter home
- Keep dogs under close control
- Consider other people

Open Access

Some routes may cross areas of land where walkers have the legal right of access under The CRoW Act 2000 introduced in May 2005. Access can be subject to restrictions and closure for land management or safety reasons for up to 28 days a year. Please respect any notices. The Countryside Council for Wales website (www.ccw.gov.uk) provides updated information on any closures.

Published by **Kittiwake**
3 Glantwymyn Village Workshops, Glantwymyn, Machynlleth, Montgomeryshire SY20 8LY
© Text & map research: Michael Burnett 2011
© Maps & illustrations: Kittiwake 2011
Drawings by Morag Perrott
Cover photos: Main – Rhaeadr Mawddach: David Perrott. *Inset* – The Coed-y-Brenin Centre: Forestry Commission Picture Library/John McFarlane

Printed by MWL, Pontypool.

ISBN: **978 1 902302 89 8**

Care has been taken to be accurate. However neither the author nor the publisher can accept responsibility for any errors which may appear, or their consequences. If you are in any doubt about access, check before you proceed.